A SEA OF LEGO & LAVENDER

A Memoir of Love, Madness and Rising from the Ashes

SARAH SMALL

A SEA OF LEGO & LAVENDER

Written by Sarah Small

Book Title: A Sea of Lego & Lavender

Dedication

For everyone who ever needed the courage to be vulnerable, an ear to listen, a shoulder to cry on, and a new beginning…xo

Since writing these pages, my feelings have softened, and my compassion for myself and all of those involved has grown. Writing was part of my grieving process on the road to acceptance and to making a new life. I wrote while still grieving the loss of the steady mental health I once took for granted, the marriage and husband I had treasured, the vocation as a lawyer I lived daily, and the blind faith to which I previously surrendered my heart's true desires.

My current memory of these events is now less visceral, and I'm grateful I preserved this sequence of events when I was still reliving it vividly. Names are amended to protect the privacy of those present through my journey – this is my retelling, and it's how I felt when it was written in 2013. It is what it is. We all have our own perspective as to how things were experienced, felt, and now fade away into the past.

Preface

Stories of survival in the face of horrendous and dehumanizing circumstances have always fascinated me. I saw them as stories that served as a testament to the power of one's faith. It amazed me how that faith, typically faith in God, coupled with the will to survive, fueled people in their darkest times. The ones that stand out to me are *"Night"* by Elie Wiesel, who survived the Holocaust, and "Left to Tell" by Immaculee Ilibagiza, who survived the Rwandan genocide. These stories showed me that horrendous circumstances are survivable.

I was raised Catholic, strict and very sheltered. I got the chance to *"be a kid."* As a teenager, I went through the sacrament of confirmation to confirm my Catholic faith. I didn't deeply consider alternatives, but figured if the dogma hadn't changed in two thousand years, it must be good. I felt at home at mass because it was part of my upbringing.

I always thought it would be my faith in God that would get me through anything. It helped me never feel lonely. When I lived in Australia and then in Italy, while studying abroad, I always went to mass. It felt like it was my home away from home. I also loved the *"Footprints"* story and figured that I, too, would be magically carried through anything.

I had a few tough times growing up. My favorite teacher, Sr. Claire, who taught me both kindergarten and third grade, died when I was in fifth grade. My dad's dad died when I was in high school. Also, during high school, a guy my dad had sentenced to jail shot and killed his own wife and friends, and we were escorted by local police to safety because he was at large with a hit list that included the local judges. I had heart surgery when I was nineteen because I was born with an extra nerve that excited instead of regulated my heartbeat. Still, despite these experiences, for me, it felt like I had not faced any real trials. I successfully graduated from university, then law school, and passed the bar. I started practicing and became a partner in my small firm nine months later. Overall, I felt like my life was lucky and charmed, a series of success stories.

Except…I always had a constant, uneasy, secret pit in the bottom of my stomach. Like my gut either sensed or was just plain afraid that I wouldn't always be lucky and that when it hit the fan, it would all come at once. A divine storm, I've heard it described. Was my feeling that of a premonition, or did my storm manifest out of my fears? Either way, I never really saw my storm coming. The birds didn't stop singing, and animals didn't head for the hills, as often occurs before natural disasters. I had no idea the disasters coming my way would be so traumatizing to me; they would seem otherworldly. My Catholic faith intensified, instead of alleviated, my inconceivable inferno. And, as it was for Dante, the only way out was through.

Winston Churchill, *"When you're going through hell, keep going."*

Right Now
(2013)

How long does it take to forgive? What does forgiveness really look like? Feel like? Betrayal, I know well. For me, it feels like healing must precede forgiveness. I'm still working on both, and it's been three years since the worst of it. I finally found a forgiveness quote that feels like it's within my reach:

"To understand everything is to forgive everything." Buddha.

To me, understanding seems a lot easier than forgiving those who contributed to what happened. If understanding and forgiving are synonymous, I'm almost there. I'll trust Buddha on that.

My wounds are so deep I don't know the actual words to describe the feelings and the darkness that is still healing. I've given myself time, therapy, travel, and now a new life out of state. Everyone has their traumas. My most recent ones were like a series of specially and personally tailored versions of hell on Earth. Yet I survived. Maybe it's still difficult for me to believe it even happened. Maybe writing it is a transmutation of the pain, to affirm it's just a story now. It's over. And I can let go by leaving it on the page.

I feel like if I never shared my story, I would be the tree that fell in the forest without making a sound. We never know what others have survived unless we share our stories. Share experiences, survival tactics, and emotions. So many things feel like they should kill us on the spot because they are so unbearable to endure. Except then, no matter how horrid it was, what comes next is up to us.

Contents

Chapter 1

THE MEET CUTE

The air was cool and wet, but it wasn't raining. I walked from my studio to the law school building. The fall of 1999 was the beginning of my first year of law school at Seattle University. I went straight from Gonzaga undergrad to Seattle U law school. I didn't have a plan for myself other than that. School was school, and I'd likely rely on my judge dad's connections to get a job. I wasn't concerned with high grades, and luckily, I soon realized that just passing didn't take much effort on my part. Classes were dull when you weren't the one getting called on. The professors called on us alphabetically, so I didn't sweat it most days. Instead of studying, I frequently went out dancing and clubbing.

Most often, I was with Bryan Moreno and some of his guy friends who graduated with their MBAs the same year that I graduated undergrad at Gonzaga. Another girl, their friend Becca, was usually with us. The guys would serve as our dance partner—or bodyguards, as the case may be. One weekend, just after I got back from spending part of my student loans to ring in Y2K in Australia, I went out four nights in a row. Thursday, Friday, Saturday, and Sunday. On the third night, the MBA guys wanted to go to a primarily Asian club. But Becca and I were both tall, at least five-foot-nine—without our heels. We didn't feel like towering over everyone in the room. Instead, she and I decided to go somewhere else, where we knew we'd have protection—from our bouncer friend Moose.

Moose was well over six feet tall and had muscles for miles. He once scooped me up by the scruff of my neck, plucking me out of the oncoming fray of a bar fight that had just broken out behind me. We knew Moose would have our backs while the guys were at "Club Asia."

I volunteered to drive. I preferred not to drink so that I'd be extra aware without our usual *"protection detail."* The club was super crowded, and from the street, I could hear the Kube 93 spinning. It was a cold night, and thankfully, we didn't have to wait long to get in. After greeting Moose, I couldn't help but notice that most of the girls had such short skirts on that their underwear was way too easily visible. At one point, I went over to the bar with Becca to get another water while she waited for her next drink. The air was warm and thick because the club was packed. It was so packed that I just continued dancing at the bar counter, not caring how far away I was from the actual dance floor.

Not paying attention, I accidentally bumped into someone behind me. To my surprise, he (I assumed he was male) bumped me back. I didn't turn around. We kept dancing, butt to butt. Once the drinks arrived, I left with Becca, and we headed back toward the real dance floor. The mystery butt sneakily followed.

From behind me, I heard, *"Why did you leave? I was having fun dancing with you?!"* His words and marshmallow-y accented voice floated across the top of my head.

I froze. I looked at Becca. Becca looked over my head. He was tall. But was he worth meeting? Before I caved in and turned around, I noiselessly mouthed to Becca, *"Is-He-Cute??"* Her jaw noticeably dropped as she speechlessly nodded: Yes.

I turned around, and Becca hadn't lied; he was tall, dark, and handsome. He introduced himself as Jasper Davies. JD was a pilot based in New York. He originally grew up in Haiti. Not to be outdone, I bragged I'd just gotten back from Australia. I'd been an exchange student there in high school and just partied through Y2K with my down-under friends. Envious because he hadn't been there before, he named about a dozen other countries he had been to in his earlier flight attendant days. I shared that I speak Italian and found out that he speaks French and Haitian Creole. After discovering that neither of us was a clear winner for *"most worldly,"* we chatted the night away. Sometimes, we held hands, but we didn't kiss because it turned out he was dating the bartender! She would take him away with her on all her smoke breaks, but he'd unapologetically always come back to taller, blonder, cuter me.

By the end of the night, his killer line was, *"I'm a pilot; I'm good with numbers. Just tell me your number, and I'll memorize it and call you."* I'd never heard that one before! And his voice and accent made it sound so smooth. I was so impressed that I gave him my correct number. The next night, as I was curling my hair to go out for the fourth night in a row, my phone rang. It was JD. I heard a bunch of horns honking in the background. He had just landed back in New York and called me from his cab ride home. I was surprised, felt special, and was even more impressed.

About a month later, the first time JD came back out to Seattle to visit me, he said he accidentally ran into the bartender at the airport. *"What are you doing here??"* she asked.

"Uh, surprise!" was his response, and he childishly snuck away from her to call me to explain.

He got caught. I laughed. I said, *"No worries. I have other dates this weekend [one was for my law school prom], but I'm single. Before I see you, I prefer that you be officially single, too."* I let him work things out and didn't see him until his next trip out.

Our first *"date,"* I think, was sometime in February. We had burgers and beer. I walked him back to his hotel because I wouldn't let him stay over at my place. Our first kiss was on the street corner and was the smelliest, worst-tasting first kiss I ever had. They inevitably got better after that. At the end of the night, before I escaped his hotel room, having only gone to second base, he tried making me stay by pointing out how good we looked together. I looked up and looked at us in the mirror, mid-embrace. My heart skipped a beat. He was right. We undeniably looked good together. I liked it too. I thought that meant something, and I kept seeing him.

A few years went by. I graduated law school, passed the bar, and got a job as expected—thanks to someone I knew through my dad. By the third year after we met, JD was visiting me about once a month. I didn't want to live with someone before marriage. Although he would stay with me, I felt better about him having his own mailbox at a mail store. He thought it was silly, but the long-distance relationship and his job made it seem sillier for him to get his apartment in Seattle instead of staying with me. The mailbox made me feel like at least one thing would change after we eventually married.

I had a strict Catholic upbringing. And my dad was a judge. For the most part, I, therefore, behaved and made choices pleasing to my parents and the church. So, it took me over three years after meeting JD to sleep with him for the first time. I finally lost my virginity to him on the Fourth of July on the Ikea couch in my TV room. I gave in against my upbringing and fears—and, as a bonus, there were fireworks, literally all around. I chose that summer of 2002 because post-9/11—and after another flight accident where a plane rolled over and crashed just after takeoff—I felt like I couldn't lose him without having shared that with him because I loved him so much. My mom taught me that someone who stayed with you when you weren't sleeping with them really loved you. I never doubted his love—he'd waited for me for over three years. As a public health nurse, she also told me each week of high school which STDs were going around, and once I saw a video of a C-section when she was teaching Lamaze, and I was just a kid. I was way too scared to have sex. I finally manned up at twenty-six, throwing caution to the wind and going for it, believing we would later get engaged and marry. That wasn't a good enough reason for the church. Later, when I confessed premarital sex to a priest at the cathedral, his reprimand-wrapped penance brought me to tears.

I was getting anxious about JD's intentions after we'd been exclusive for over three years, and I was planning to break up with him if we weren't engaged by August of 2004. I didn't see any point in continuing if we weren't moving forward.

That May, he took me to the Dominican Republic for a vacation. We had picked out a diamond together at a shop we heard about from a friend. I didn't know if he was ready to propose, though, and all week, we were enjoying the sights of the island and he kept saying he wasn't ready. I finally sighed and told him if he wasn't ready, don't do it. I had searched his bag while he was in the shower, and I didn't find the ring. I wondered if he was serious about not being ready. I gave up hope. On the last night, we talked to my parents. I remember getting ready to go to a beach party. Each night, we took a walk on the beach before going to bed, and we walked before the party. Tired and hopeless, I was ready to leave the party early and head back to the room. Instead, he asked me to take one more walk.

The sun was already down, and as we walked by the water and away from the party, he suddenly got down on one knee. I was instantly speechless. "Sarah Lorraine Small, will you marry me?" I nodded and managed to whisper *"yes"* as tears rolled down my cheeks. I found out he wasn't *"ready"* because he had to talk to my dad to get permission first. Apparently, they were back home at a card party, waiting to hear from us with the good news. I probably spent the next year working as much on wedding preparations as I did on my billable hours.

Chapter 2

THE LAST SUPPER

Married life was much like dating JD. He was usually away flying, eventually even overseas. I was usually working, or hanging out with friends to avoid being home and feeling alone. We had a small, three-bedroom house and SUV for the future children. When they didn't arrive, we started with a little dog, something I could love when JD was away. Quality time together was rare, and I valued it like a treasure. One night, he cooked Haitian. It smelled wonderful and instantly relaxed me as I walked through the back door of the garage. It had been a long day at the office. I always worked extra hard to bill as many hours as I could to give me the freedom to spend a few days off each month during the ten-day window that flying cargo allowed him to be home finally. JD had cooked rice and beans, fried plantains, and spiced baked chicken… he had even already set the table, which was usually my job. I didn't even smell burnt rice, as his skills in the kitchen were improving. Being Haitian and having been raised on the islands, he loved eating his own home cooking. There was only one Haitian restaurant in the Seattle area, but it was an hour's drive away, and it didn't taste as good as JD's cooking eventually did unless we wanted griyo—a special fried pork dish.

The mustard yellow walls of the kitchen and dining area were glowing; I assumed it was the warmth of the paint color and a little of the warmth of his love that was going into his cooking that night. Little did I know it was really an energetic spilling over of white-hot guilt that was blazing inside him.

I don't remember if I changed clothes or just removed my suit jacket. Having been at the office on a day he was home must have meant I had court or client meetings and dressed the part. I remember being eager not only for food but for the company of my husband, who had just worked two back-to-back schedules and hadn't been home in a long time. Once we sat down and before he prayed so we could begin eating, I began to pick up on his unusual mood. Instead of starting a prayer, he had an announcement.

He informed me, while bowing his head and sitting there more like a kid than a six-foot-four grown man that this would be his *"last supper."* At times, I teased him for being a *"drama king,"* but this certainly didn't sound like the opportunity for a joke. English being his second language, he often confused metaphors and used words in his own special way. For example, it took me awhile to notice that *"cute"* to him meant *"nice"* in the context of his speech. I would tell him about something nice a friend did for me, and he would say, *"Aw, that's cute."* But *"Last Supper"* didn't have its special meaning. I tried to take it in. What in the world did he intend that to mean? I was completely confused. Clueless, I didn't know how to react or what to say. I sat motionless in my chair. I couldn't even pick up my fork.

Next, he made his full confession. I somewhat foggily recall hearing something like, *"I slept with two prostitutes in Hong Kong in July."* (However, he later recanted, instead saying he was drugged and roofied by two prostitutes in Hong Kong, and he didn't know for sure what happened. Later, his story evolved into, *"I slept with two Australian girls, who are now my friends on Facebook."*

And that he'd slept with others; he said previously he'd "only kissed." I accept that I will never know the truth, but it was clear, whatever the means, that his vows were not intact.) My insides dropped. They dropped so far I couldn't even feel them anymore. In fact, my insides were no longer inside me but somewhere in the earth's core... I was one hundred percent stunned. Shell-shocked. To me, the confession was an atomic bomb, and my chair at the kitchen table was ground zero. I still sat immobile and speechless, unable to process or react. I was usually so good in crisis, at least when it called for helping others. Personal tragedy was entirely alien to me.

When, like one having recovered from a traumatic brain injury, I rediscovered my ability to speak, my first question tumbled out of my mouth. It was so simple I might as well have spelled it out across the table in alphabet letter blocks. *"What do you want?"* He hardly hesitated before saying quietly, *"I don't know."* I could barely look at him, so I looked slightly over him as he spoke. Above his head was the mini-reproduction souvenir of Botticelli's *Madonna and Child* that I had reproduced in fresco form. If JD felt he was at his Last Supper and awaiting his crucifixion, was I, like Mary, to stand by him?

Our dinner went uneaten. The rest of our words, now jumbled by memory, involved something like me asking for a more detailed account. His detailed account involved him starting the illustrious night out at a bar with other pilots, a strip club of sorts before he wakes up next to used condoms, not remembering or whatever. My first instinct was to discover what he wanted, my way of trying to decode the meaning of his actions. Meanwhile, how I felt about it or what I might want because of his transgressions truly hadn't even crossed my mind. Not even a minuscule flutter! No synapses fired on those subjects.

Because of my religious upbringing, I believed I had no power to undo or abandon the bonds of the sacrament of marriage.

Having married a pilot, I had anticipated and intensely feared this possibility deep, deep, deep down, and had preemptively decided that I was capable of forgiveness, no matter how difficult. Because I loved him and because the bonds were unbreakable, I anticipated an eventual reconciliation.

Still, it was no wonder, some seven years into our relationship, that he disclosed a transgression like cheating. I really should have seen it coming because he'd practically cheated on the girl he was dating when we met the first time he came back to Seattle to visit me.

I was admittedly out of my league. I didn't know what was happening or what would happen. I suggested, and he agreed that we seek out professional assistance, and within days, we saw a marriage counselor. Before he went back to work, our counselor suggested I get all my questions answered. My approach was to sit him back down at the kitchen table. I put his French version of the Bible in his left hand and swore him under oath before making him recount every dirty detail. It didn't make me feel better in the least, but I think it shook him up, and I enjoyed that because he'd shaken me to my core.

Still, in that moment, face to face with that disclosure, what did I do? Well. I certainly couldn't eat. The smell and remnants of the Last Supper instantly turned foul. One thing I knew, I didn't want him to touch me. In a kind of *"auto-response,"* I suggested we start counseling. It often seemed to me, though, that couples who required counseling rarely recovered. I felt like counseling was the next logical step, but I didn't believe it could fix our issues. The damage was done. I recently saw an article with a photograph of damaged fine porcelain that, according to Japanese tradition, had been repaired with gold instead of superglue. Neither were available to fill in our breakage. He got so angry when I flinched at him and automatically moved away from his touch. Finally, having found the will to stand in the kitchen, I couldn't let him touch me. I would surely have crumbled.

I needed a time-out, a total escape, or to wake up from my black-and-white TV show life that had, over the course of one supper, become a full-color, feature-length nightmare. JD paced angrily on the other side of the counter while I remained sheltered behind the sink, stumbling through additional conversation until it was decided that he would sleep upstairs. If we had a doghouse his size, I would have preferred the literal interpretation, but up he went. One floor separated us, him suspended above.

I don't know how or if I slept that night. I needed to cry, and I'm not sure if I did. I probably didn't. When I was little, maybe six, I remember crying about something until my mom sternly said, *"Do you feel better now??"* I tearfully looked up, and gave the response she was obviously looking to hear, *"No," sniff, tear*. *"Well then, why are you crying?"* she replied, a matter of fact. I learned early on that crying was more a sign of weakness instead of a healthy form of self-soothing. Feelings, especially expressing them, and vulnerability were shameful activities. It was better to be *"tough." "I'm just toughening you up,"* Dad would say when I returned from my room after another private cry from being teased, probably called a *"walking hormone."* Whenever I needed a cry under their roof, I turned not to their arms for comfort but to a stuffed elephant. He was mostly charcoal gray, and he held all my childhood tears. The night of the Last Supper, I just tried to sleep. I would rather have died than share the truth, which would have been required to reach out for third-party comfort.

After I got up, I went to the bathroom to start my day as usual. I washed my face and put my contacts in, praying that the routine might offer me a tiny bit of comfort. But when I looked up at myself in the bathroom mirror, I got scared. My eyes had gone lifeless and dull. No light reflected from them, not one little sparkle. Then I started to feel. And how I felt was soul-broken, not just heart-broken. I had been all in. I put more than one hundred percent of my blind faith into our love, the vows, and God. I believed my daily prayers for JD would strengthen him and help him be the better man he constantly told me he longed to be. He said he wanted to be a stronger Christian and more disciplined in his faith and health practices on the road, more present with me at home. He had always proclaimed his Christianity. Where was his Baptist upbringing now? He'd have to answer for this, not just to me…but to God. Would God set him straight? Had he meant the vows on our wedding day, or did he just want to mean them? If he meant them, then when did he change his mind? Or was he not capable of them, regardless of his true intent? The altar had been a guillotine in disguise for me because it turned out that I had no capacity for coping with betrayal.

I thought back to when JD got home in August of 2010, and he refused to kiss me. I'd acquiesced to that before. He said he was *"sick,"* even though I observed no actual symptoms. No cough, sniffle, or fever. Like he had on past occurrences, he promised that he didn't want to get me sick. Like all the other times, I said I didn't care. Still, he refused. How many times had he done that? Now that I knew it was because he had just been with someone else… I began reaching back into my closet of memories to distinguish how often he'd come home refusing to kiss me due to no apparent sickness. How often had I thought, how sweet, he's being overly cautious to protect me? For how long had he been cheating? How often? Under oath, he feebly disclosed that sometimes he would just kiss or make out with someone, but I knew he wasn't fully disclosing everything to me. It would have meant facing himself, not just me.

I could not compute. Could not *"recalculate"* as I hovered about my life in an unmapped zone on GPS. I wanted to disappear. Not take my own life, but magically disappear. Pain over. The stress of that traumatic revelation caused my body to give out on me. First, I couldn't sleep, then I could hardly function. I tried running, wearing myself out again and again to the Twilight soundtrack on the treadmill at the YMCA. Sweating it out instead of crying it out, hoping that sweaty saltwater could substitute for tears that still escaped me. It wasn't enough. I tried to run myself into exhaustion, into sleep. My body wouldn't play along.

We immediately tried a few more counseling sessions, but I didn't feel any relief. He was upset we didn't have kids, didn't have zero debt, didn't have his dream job, or a bigger, cleaner house. Accused me of *"taking him to the cleaners."* Didn't I clear his old debts, the ones he had been paying, when there was no legal obligation to do so? Didn't I clear his record so that he could get hired as a 747 captain? Do over half the work of his online four-year degree? Consistently work since we'd met? Been open to fertility treatments when we discovered his swimmers were too kinky to swim? My Catholic upbringing had led me to believe the only way out of marriage was death. I had to stay. I didn't know how to handle the situation, so I continued to consult with *"professionals."* A counselor. Then, a doctor.

All I knew for sure was I wanted my family to stay out of it. I only knew my parents and siblings to be the mathematical inverse of compassionate, nonjudgmental types. I needed the autonomy and freedom to attempt reconciliation without their interference and judgment. I was embarrassed, too. How could this happen to me? How could he do this to me? A good, honest, faithful, loving Christian wife? I felt I had done nothing but support him, pray for him, and try to live up to his expectations. Hah. In that vein, I was the tree. The giving tree. And how would this tree stand up at my brother's wedding, which was about a week away from JD's Last Supper? How? Without breaking down? How do you break without breaking? You don't. I soon learned that there are pills for a lot of things, but there are no pills for that.

Chapter 3

LAVENDER HAZE

Ironically, just beyond my marital wreckage was my brother's wedding. It was scheduled for about a week after the Last Supper. I was horrified that I was to be a bridesmaid and JD a groomsman. We were to walk the aisle together, and it felt like it would be an impossible feat under the new circumstances. I'm sure it was expected that I would practically skip at his side all the way down the aisle, feeling warm and fuzzy with memories of our wedding. My whole family, especially my parents, were uber-Catholic. But JD had just committed adultery.

This *"Little Red"* had discovered she married the *"wolf."* It terrified me to come to terms with that because I still loved who I thought he was, I still subscribed to those vows to the death, and I prayed for reconciliation to avoid family judgment. I was more terrified of their judgment and their interference with my autonomy to process and decide how to handle the situation than I was of the wolf, which I, however upsettingly, still loved.

My sister had just married in May and, already, it was my brother's turn. In between I'd also been in my girlfriend Amy's wedding in July, which JD wasn't home for. The first wedding I attended that year was my former roommate's, for which I'd gone all the way to Tampa, working there and back to keep up. It was in a year full of weddings that I learned my marriage had disintegrated.

To create an escape hatch where I would have the space I needed, although not the support I now know I needed more, I had to think of something. How the hell would I not let on what I'd learned? Hide what was happening. To me, there was no way to be a no-show. I honestly don't think it even occurred to me to call my brother and tell him I wouldn't be there. That would certainly lead to a breakdown, which was not an option. Because then my parents would know. Even then, I felt reconciling with JD was not an option—and they knew they would never look at JD the same way again, to the point that we'd practically have to move overseas, or at least away. I felt it wouldn't have been fair to him, and it wouldn't have been fair to me, either, to involve them. How many times did I hear, growing up, that *"life isn't fair"*? Their classic answer to my constant disgruntled attitude toward all shapes, sizes, and colors of injustices. It even formed the basis of my law school application essay, where I explained that becoming a lawyer would help me make life fair for others. So there, Mom and Dad.

Unfortunately, the only escape from fear I knew to work was little and round and easy to swallow. I'd had countless traumatic childhood experiences at the hands of a dentist who had a nose like Pinocchio and one half-finger due to an incident with the underbelly of a lawnmower. Each time I had to go back to him, I was more afraid. Each time I was more afraid, it required more Novocaine to numb me, and half-finger's patience grew more and more thin. There was always a toy in the special drawer waiting for me, but each time my tears dried and I took a toy, I felt I deserved the whole drawer for what they had just put me through. Most times, my mom would have to come in and sooth me, but she usually wouldn't stay for the whole thing because my fear made the procedure take so long and because he needed the space by my chair for him and his assistant to surround and torture me. I was like the guy in the game of Operation who isn't let free when he vibrates with pain, and you just try again on your next turn. To this day, just the sound of the drill puts me on the ceiling. Before my wedding, I had four cavities that needed attention. I told the dentist I'd wait until I was on JD's dental insurance to get them done. Really, I was scared to death. My dentist had all his fingers and a large, perfect, pearly white smile like the Cheshire Cat. It was all I could see through the sunglasses they made me wear in the chair. When I finally succumbed to an appointment for a filling, I shared how scared I was. He offered me Valium. He was shocked I hadn't said something sooner about my fears. I used to freak all of them out as they worked on my mouth while I white-knuckled the arms of the chair, tears slowly rolling down the sides of my face, in and over my ears, to the floor. Valium. It just meant I needed a ride to and from the appointments whenever drilling was required. By the time this was sorted, I required seven fillings, one redo of a root canal, and two crowns. But before and after those appointments, I, too, smiled like the Cheshire Cat because when I was on Valium, I'd be happy for the sky to fall. I'd even giggle in Chicken Little's face.

Days before the wedding, I called my general practitioner and made an appointment. Through a waterfall of tears and explanation, I demanded enough pills to get through the entire rehearsal dinner and wedding day. She prescribed twenty.

We wore lavender. It's my sister-in-law's favorite color, and it's even the color of the sapphire she chose instead of a diamond engagement ring. The night before, I'd taken four Valiums, two before and two during the rehearsal dinner. JD drove, and I slept in the car on the way there. He was stunned that I finally slept. I was grateful for the rest my body desperately needed and relieved when I was able to keep up a Valium-induced façade the entire rehearsal dinner. But the dinner was a few hours, whereas the wedding was a whole day... The day of the wedding, my best friend floated around in lavender with me, dispensing Valium as if from a PEZ dispenser whenever I seemed to well up a bit, but pre-tears. Which meant I, over the day, consumed the other sixteen happy pills.

The only memories I have of the wedding mass are repeated, desperate, fleeting thoughts about whether any of the talk about marriage and vows during the ceremony had any impact whatsoever on JD. Then, I'm at the reception in a hall that I guess was a community center/gym because I vaguely recall basketball hoops from the ceiling. Besides lavender, the theme was Lego. Yes, the toy bricks. The bombonieri were tiny bags of Lego brick-shaped candy. My brother's gift to his bride was a Lego brick Death Star that he'd prebuilt all by himself. I was popping Valium in a sea of Lego and lavender, trying to avoid the man I'd promised my heart to for a lifetime.

Was my brother happy? Was his bride pretty? I think so, but really, I don't remember. Did I dance with my brother? I have no idea.

There was one elevator ride at the end of the evening where I nearly fell over when it started moving. My mom commented, *"Somebody's on something,"* while Jennah and I just giggled. I had taken Valium at my sister's wedding a few months prior, but only one pill to take the edge off. Mom even had one after we lost Grandpa that day. He was in the early stages of Alzheimer's. He was lost, and she was losing it. Both required attention. I talked her into a Valium before hunting Papa down. Of course, he wasn't run over by a car and hadn't even left the building. It turned out he was perfectly fine, having ordered himself a mini buffet at the Washington Athletic Club restaurant. He forgot he had already eaten. So, my mom wasn't surprised when I was obviously on something at my brother's wedding, and she added in the elevator,

"Someone should lay off the drugs." Little did she know I had taken about sixteen Valiums throughout the day, then drank myself to oblivion and was sick in the WAC sports bar bathroom before JD and I finally made it up to our room.

There was no way I would disclose my sky was falling. Admitting it openly would have made it more painfully real, and I was overwhelmed with the secret knowledge, unable to bear more. Valium kept my Chicken Little's terrified cry deep within me.

Chapter 4

RETURN TO ST. JAMES

Before JD went back to work, I remember us going to mass once at the St. James Cathedral in Seattle, where we were married. It was as if we both longed for a reboot, the ability to return to that day and start over. We found seats behind where we'd knelt and taken our vows the weekend after Easter—and the day that Pope John Paul II had died—on April 2, 2005. Our wedding preceded the pope's memorial mass that day. We were on three television stations. I still have the video footage and the radio coverage, too, along with the two-DVD set of our wedding video, complete with illustrated credits, love story, best wishes from friends and family, and reception footage where, before we eat, his father says a blessing in French as his uncle translates.

Except that day when he and I were at mass, there were no leftover Easter flowers. It felt spooky to me sitting in that northern section, facing what would have been our backs as we knelt and then stood to take our vows just over five years prior. Since we began dating, JD attended mass with me even though he was raised Baptist. He loved the organ music, so he seemed to look forward to the cathedral services. I would line up for communion as he stayed seated. Going back and remembering our wedding ceremony, instead of coming back from communion, I wanted to run out the side door and let him wonder where I was. I wondered what he would do if I disappeared. Instead, I stopped over at the side statue of the Madonna and Child near the exit to light a candle and say a prayer. Only one word came to me. *"Help."* It was all I could come up with. Often, my prayers were ones of gratitude, not requests. I looked up. Mary was holding Jesus. They looked down and back at me. *"Do Not Be Afraid"* flashed through my mind. I got an answer. A message I had heard before. Had I heard it before so that I'd be able to recall it at this very moment?

The first delivery of that message came while I was living in Florence, studying at my university's campus there. At that time, Gonzaga-in-Florence was located at Palazzo Antinori, much closer to the Duomo than the school's current location on Via della Pira. I lived at Hotel Ottaviani, a few steps from Santa Maria Novella, not far from the main train station. Only six of us students lived at small Hotel Ottaviani, and it took up the second and third floors of the building, which started at floor zero. Many stairs above, just past the reception desk, and next door to the dining room decorated with Fr. Bruno paintings, was my room. Eva and I shared room number five, where, on my drunkest night, I lost my room keys, only to find them still hanging out in the door's outer keyhole. However, I was sober when I remember waking up in the middle of the night to what felt like my cold, dead body.

Totally cold. Totally immovable. I freaked. I panicked but couldn't move. In an instant, warm, bright light started piercing through my body until I practically became pure light, hovering above my pensione twin bed. All I remember hearing was: *Do not be afraid*. All I remember seeing was Mary holding a child, Jesus. Whether that was an image in the light or my projection onto the light based on what I heard and believed as a Catholic, I'm not sure. Then I woke up. I was totally fine but totally shaken. I didn't tell anyone but my journal at first, wondering what it was that made me special enough to have that kind of experience in the first place. I was too scared to ask if others had ever experienced something similar.

Hearing the *"Do not be afraid"* message again that day in the cathedral was like the gold nugget of hope I'd been panning for. Grandma and Papa used to love panning for gold. I took my nugget, but it was way easier said than done as I and life as I knew it was soon washed away in a tsunami of uncertainty.

Chapter 5

PRESCRIBED INTO A RABBIT HOLE

JD went back to work. With one family event down, there was still a weeklong mother-daughter horse trip around the corner in September. Plus, I had a law office to run, cases to handle, court appearances to make, and clients with whom I had to meet. And with JD out of town again a day or two after the wedding, right back to Hong Kong, the scene of the crime, I was left alone. Alone, Valium-less. Sleeplessness was closing in on me like a fog of darkness that ever so slowly creeps in until you're surrounded, with no room for escape. I might as well have become Minnie in my own thriller version of *Fantasia*...

Like a zombie, I went to my office daily. I still wasn't doing any work, but that was where my assistant Sophie kept me company. Other than Jennah, she was the only person I'd told that JD had cheated. I broke down and told Jennah just after a hot yoga class because I knew she'd instantly be on my side. Besides, she knew how to keep a secret, and she knew my parents. She had worked for my dad in his court, where she had been brought to tears by his personally oblivious insensitivity, as had my former law partner, who was his former court clerk. My father believes he just speaks and does the truth and justice. He and his pride make no apologies, especially if you're just not tough enough to take it.

Sophie heard me bawling at my desk the day after JD confessed. I'd gone in because I didn't know where else to go or what else to do as if I could find some solace in my routine. I was relieved that she knew because she was and is shit, the person who not only has your back in a bar fight but who jumps over you and onto the person you're up against, taking them down with the fierceness and agility of a winged monkey.

Sophie knew I still hadn't slept, so that I wouldn't be doing any work, and she rearranged my schedule. I was taking Benadryl, which at first put me down for six hours, then four, then two, then none. Then, after almost a week of little to no sleep, I went back to my doctor for the next quick fix. I told her about the sleeplessness and my desperation. For starters, she gave me Ambien CR. Regular Ambien helps you fall asleep. I insisted that I needed not just to fall asleep but to stay asleep. I needed to function again. She obliged, hardly hesitating to prescribe the Ambien CR. My tears won her over. Alternate options weren't even discussed. I texted JD from the office pharmacy as an FYI/in-your-face message. What I really wanted to message him was, *"You caused me to need drugs just to sleep."* My empty bag of coping skills was equally at fault, if not more, and he had his own issues, but I was not myself. I just let him know what was prescribed and that I'd start taking it that night. The insert listing the side effects seemed to open like five feet of scroll. It described a bunch of things that I would possibly not even be aware of myself. I didn't have JD or anyone at home to monitor me, but on the thirteenth floor, where my office was located, Sophie had eyes on me, at least in the daytime.

Desperate and exhausted, I started taking the Ambien CR. The first night I slept almost the full seven hours it promised, although I still felt a little out of it. I needed way more sleep than that to catch up on all the missed hours. The next night, though, I only got five. Then three, then one, then…none.

In the meantime, on the road to rebound insomnia, I was sleep-driving and sleep-shopping. The things I was doing felt like dreaming, but they actually happened, like filling more than my car with purchases late at night at Walmart, a twenty-four-hour store where the clerk offered to put the remaining purchases in his car and follow me home to unload them. I met Tyler while standing in the outdoor aisle looking at bird accessories, happily being reminded of my grandma and thinking about coloring a garden stone with a bird picture on it for her. I also remembered I had been upset that JD hadn't liked my birdfeeder in the backyard because the leftover seed grew surprises around its base. Tyler was probably nineteen, and I thought he had every tattoo I would have had if I had tattoos. One was of his childhood dog. I would have Schnoodle, our Schnauzer-poodle, who was like my other little brother, who we dressed in pajamas and grew up with. I thought my dad had so coolly and cleverly named until I grew up and realized that combining Schnauzer with poodle was the simple, later obvious, basis of his name. But I was the kid who played along with Grandpa when he told me they punch the holes in Swiss cheese and have been teased to this day for having believed it. My denial of having not known meant nothing to my parents. Not realizing Schnoodle's name wasn't radically creative went along with how they saw me.

After opening a Walmart store card to fill the house with items I thought I'd need during an extended break from work—and to start a new life with new things with the person with whom I hoped to reconcile—I went to Target the next night and did the same. I might have even gotten a flu shot because my mom later found fliers about them in the dozens of red dot-circled bags. They, too, gave me a store card. I'd spent over a thousand combined, but the monthly payments were minuscule, and I planned on an extended leave being necessary to recoup from the blow. I wanted to be surrounded by happy things and fun projects and even to get more dogs. Teddy had become my dog since I was the only one home, so JD needed one or more of his own to fulfill his whole *"hot wife coming to pick him up at the end of Boeing Field as he walks toward her in his UPS-brown captain's uniform toward the Land Rover with his kids in the back, big dogs in the way back"* fantasy.

After about a week on Ambien, Sophie didn't know about the sleep-shopping, but she readily reported that I looked like shit. She told me to go back to the doctor, who'd become my apothecary with all the answers. She told me to ask for antidepressants, which she figured I would need—I might as well get ahead of the game.

Back at my doctor's office, I described the problems I was still having with sleep, plus there was that upcoming mother-daughter horse trip I was expected to attend. I literally asked what combination of pills would make me behave like nothing was wrong for a whole week with my mom. This time, my personal apothecary came through even bigger. I waited in the pharmacy to pick up two new friends and one old. Celexa, lorazepam, and Valium came to Mad Hatter's party that Ambien CR had already gotten started.

Jennah came over that Labor Day weekend, again serving up pills as if they were PEZ but watching in horror as I deteriorated. She couldn't keep up with me. I was journaling my dreams and feelings, sharing them with her while talking faster than would seem humanly possible. I was seeing dead people before I fell asleep. They wanted my help. One wanted to tell me a story about a train. I heard the train. I'd watched the show on television where kids see ghosts, and adults help them learn to tell them to go away. I told them to leave me alone. Instead, I fell asleep, thinking I was dying. The hallucinations were causing panic attacks. When I had an attack in the red-stalled bathroom at the movies, Jennah gave me a lorazepam, which kept me feeling safe through the movie

Eat, Pray, Love, which had me laughing hysterically to the point of embarrassing my friend, who shrank next to me in her red velvet seat. The lorazepam wore off by the time we got home. She needed to sleep before going back to work, and she ran home, leaving me to my friendly hallucination-causing and thwarting capsules of wonderland.

I thought *Eat, Pray, Love* was a great idea, and I was still comfortable driving around close to home. I went out to purchase a copy for each family member and Jennah, too. I picked up the soundtrack while I was at it. I am big into soundtracks. I pulled out my single CD boombox, set it on the kitchen bar counter that I'd later graffiti with Sharpie, and pressed repeat, letting the soundtrack fill the house all day long. Sitting at the kitchen table where JD's confession first pierced my heart, I wrote out a letter to each recipient on a yellow legal pad, which I then copied at the mailbox store. I got padded envelopes and addressed each of them. The letter closed with an invitation for them to meet me in Bali because I was off to Italy and India on my own, but we should each find our way to finally living from our hearts. I don't think the packages ended up being sent—maybe I gave some of them out in person before I spun out to the next thing.

I had to make one other envelope, more important than the rest. In case I didn't meet with him, I ended up trusting my brother to deliver this one. It was related to some bizarre dreams that were political in nature. My internal need for peace was somehow pushed to a global level in my subconscious. I dreamt something about soldiers from either side of the lines meeting or exchanging letters with each other. This exchange, set to happen soon, would be the catalyst that ended the conflicts in the East. I scribbled everything down on my legal pad after waking up. It was clear from my dream that I was to write the information I'd gathered from the dream and deliver it to my local priest at St. Andrew's. I was critical to the peace process. If he didn't get my notes, and they weren't transferred up his chain of command to the right people at the Vatican, then the potential for peace would be forever lost.

In my big-time sleep-deprived-plus-prescription-altered state, I began to believe I was one of the chosen youths because of my experience in my little room in the pensione years before. It meant something, and I was part of something secret and big. I put together my package for Father Dan.

Feeling like my brain, together with all logic and reality, had moved to a new neighborhood whose ZIP code fell somewhere on the moon, something in me knew the pills were no good, and I quit them cold turkey. I finally called my brother for help, and I even told him what I had been prescribed and what I had taken (although not what happened) so that he knew why I was so out of it when he picked me up. He walked into the house, and I noticed the ring on his finger. *"You're married?!"* I exclaimed. He probably shook his head. In the car ride on the way to the airport, I told him my brain felt like the *"blue screen of death"*—exactly like I had always complained to him about my computer at my old office. I asked him to play classical music to slow my head down because it felt like everything was spinning out of control. The classical music played on as his black Ford Escape that he bought off Dad safely took us northbound to the airport. He stayed calm, let me rattle off at warp speed, and offered his idea to remedy the situation. He said he'd helped diagnose his wife, and this group of psychiatrists could help me, too.

Letting his suggestion fly in one ear and straight out the other, I suddenly wanted to know if he was one of the chosen youths too because there was one other experience we both had in Italy, and I figured it would be expected that siblings might be called to work together. Without wanting to fully disclose my theory that he may or may not be aware of, I asked him: *"Did you eat cookies?"* We had an ongoing inside joke for years that if he said yes, then he was CIA. He laughed, but then I took a different angle because that wasn't what I was really getting at. I reminded him of our trip to the Vatican. I told him about my experience at the Vatican. We were on the edge of the huge oval piazza in front of St. Peter's on our way to the Vatican Museum. It was a kind of Italian youth day, and crowds of youth were gathered in the center, but the edges were open, and few people were on the outer side of what looked like a pathway for the Popemobile. Our small group of Gonzaga students lined up along the barriers just as Pope John Paul II rode by, waving and smiling. I waved back, and as he passed, even made eye contact. It was magical. It moved me to tears to see the sparkle of life shine from his eyes.

In the car on the way to the airport, I asked Jason if he'd made eye contact, too, all those years ago. A tear rolled down his cheek as he admitted he had. Now, I don't know if he was as moved as I was or just scared of how messed up I sounded. Either way, I had my confirmation that he, too, might be joining me on a future quest. For the moment, I trusted him with my envelope for Father Dan, sensing deep down that something would prevent me from delivering it myself. He swore to get it to Father Dan's hands, and we continued northbound on Highway 167.

Instead of meeting the Infiniti SUV driven by his slightly-overweight-but-pretending-to-be-happy-with-life wife, Teddy, in the back, JD met his brother-driving-me-to-him wife, who demanded to ride home in a limo because I had great news to share with him. I told him I thought we were pregnant because what else but the hormones could cause me to act so bizarrely? And what else but a pregnancy could cause him not to leave me? That would have made our decision to stay together easy, an obvious answer gonging in the resounding dark and silent land of *"Would we stay together and, if not, how would I survive?"* I named our limo driver India because he was from India, and he went along with it because he was so entertained by my animated but strangely altered state. JD tried staying calm, and we made it home. He then reached out to Sophie, who reached out to my parents, who she thought I was close to because she was aware that we spent a lot of time together. She also knew I didn't want them to know about the cheating, but she really had no idea they were the number one people on earth I was trying to avoid.

Chapter 6

DUPED INTO THE MENTAL WARD

The things my parents were about to do to me, though in the vein of helping me, made a couple of the childhood traumas that had previously haunted me pale in comparison.

First, I was about five. We were visiting my aunt, uncle, and cousins in San Diego. It was the first time I ever flew on a plane, a Pacific Southwest Airlines plane with a big black nose and a smile painted on it. It was hard to be afraid of that smiling plane. I happily boarded with visions of Disney characters dancing in my head. We stayed with my dad's older sister, Aunt Grace, her husband, and three cousins. At some point, we visited a petting zoo. I had never seen so many different types of animals before. We didn't even have a dog.

My parents pet the animals, showing me there was nothing to be afraid of. I got into it. I started feeding a goat, careful to keep my fingers out of his mouth. But with my attention focused on the one I was feeding, another one snuck up on me from behind and started gnawing at my jacket. I freaked out, freed myself from his nibble, and ran toward safety. But no one was around. They'd all left the goat pen. I was alone. With the mean, hungry goats. I broke down into tears. No one to comfort me from the goat attack, and now I was double-traumatized at having been left behind. A nice lady came over to me and helped guide me outside the goat pen, and my family became visible. I was relieved but still tearful. They laughed. My dad laughed.

As if saying, what's the big deal? It was just a goat and we were right here all along. We didn't really leave you. Invalidating my feelings and offering no comfort. I think my aunt hugged me, and I'm sure whatever she said, she called me sweetie. She is Dad's only sibling, but their relationship was never close. Our nuclear family, plus grandma and grandpa (later named Papa because my sister couldn't pronounce grandpa), were the main players. For years, we were required to do what felt like everything together. We even had weekly family TV nights to watch *The Cosby Show* and be teased by Dad whenever our like-character did something like us. So, we got teased for their behavior, not just ours. As I looked at his blurry face through my tears, he justified his teasing as making us *"tough."*

Second, I was more like eight. Maybe even nine or ten. It was Apple Blossom, the festival in our small town of Wenatchee, that celebrated our self-proclaimed crown of being the *"Apple Capital of the World."* Apple Blossom involved a Ridge to River race. For a couple of years, we cheered my dad as he competed, canoeing under the Wenatchee River Bridge into the Columbia River water. We were also expected to participate in the *"kiddie"* parade a week before the main parade. I hated being in front of people, but we got to trade our ribbon for an ice cream bar at the end, and that was incentive enough for me.

Still, I felt like part of a moving exhibit of perfect, well-behaved children as we wore our St. Joseph's school T-shirts and waved at the parade watchers. My grandma always cheered the loudest, with Papa smiling alongside her. The following weekend was the main parade, where all the royalty would take the route with marching bands—every year was straight out of a Norman Rockwell painting. We always reserved our front-row seats by leaving picnic table benches along the route near my dad's law office for easy parking and bathroom access. Grandma made everyone in the parade feel like a celebrity as she cheered them all on. Her cheer was contagious, as she got me and even neighboring parade viewers more into it. Along came the Seattle Seafair float and surrounding Vikings.

Cheering with Grandma, and with no reason to have a guard up, I was waving. Out of nowhere, one of the Vikings, who seemed taller than my six-foot-five dad, grabbed me. Like a sack of potatoes, he flung me over his shoulder and continued the route, waving to the crowd. I was scared out of my mind. I remember looking back at my family moving up and down as he walked. They were laughing. Laughing and waving. I began kicking, physically demanding to be let down. When my obvious distress didn't lead to his release or my family's rescue, I resorted to tears. The big oaf finally got it and quickly returned me to my laughing parents, but hopefully ashamed his prank had gone wrong. It traumatized the fuck out of a helpless little girl who was taught to never leave with a stranger unless they gave the secret code: green apples. My grandma consoled me this time, but the damage was done.

How many times in therapy have I gone back, hugged my little girl self, scolded my parents, and brought the girl to the present day with me to show her that "everything's going to be alright, everything's already alright"? It was the same song Diego in Bali would later lead me at the start of my first acro-yoga class, resulting in two inversions using trustworthy men to base me as I flew. Finding my voice and the courage to be vulnerable in my family always felt like a Sisyphean feat.

I hated chocolate ice cream and sugar cones. But that was all my parents ordered for us when we went out to Baskin-Robbins or the occasional stop in Leavenworth. Crying one time because

I was about to get a chocolate scoop on a sugar cone once again, my dad took notice. He encouraged me to taste rainbow sherbet, one of his other favorites. I was overjoyed. It was my new favorite on a regular cone. It was not until years later, when I was old enough to drive myself to Baskin-Robbins that I discovered my real favorite to be chocolate chip mint.

In my adulthood, JD's cheating became the catalyst of my deepest fears of abandonment and helplessness, being relived over and over and over as events unfurled, according to Hitchcock on Crack. I would have needed Dali, Miro, Chagall, and Klimt to collaborate on a picture of my Wonderland Inferno.

JD was home, and he was seeing what a wreck he made me. My disintegrated state was traumatizing him as much as he had traumatized me, and in a small way, I felt vindicated. Wishing I could sleep, I lay alone in bed but left our bedroom door slightly open. I overheard JD talking to my parents on the phone. He had confiscated my phone, so I wasn't able to call anyone for help or any other reason. I was a mess, and he was intent on keeping me quiet to protect him and me. To me, it seemed as if he, in part, was trying to protect my law practice so I could quickly be fixed with my ability to make money intact. He wouldn't let me sabotage my cases or let anyone discover that I was not well.

JD came into our bedroom. I was lying down in the dark, and the hallway light spilled into the room when he opened the door. I was supposed to be sleeping, but sleep still escaped me. He suggested I shower. I think he meant to keep me safely occupied and wanted me to look more put together by the time my parents arrived three hours later. He hardly slept the night before; I'd made him give me a lengthy massage. I hoped he could massage my pain away, but the abdominal pain remained. I made him listen to me recounting the stories of my clients, purging the sadness that I'd carried inside far too long. He was used to a manual in the cockpit that predetermined his response in any flight emergency. In this case, there was no manual. There was no prescribed method to fix your overmedicated and heartbroken wife.

One of his Haitian friends had suggested an island-style cure for my desperation. He said JD should cover my head in raw ground meat. JD told his friend he would do it. Really, he couldn't even bring himself to buy the meat. On some level, he seemed to know what I needed was beyond his capacity to give at that point. He also knew backup was on the way.

They weren't so much coming to rescue me, but my parents were driving over to rescue JD, who was at a loss for what to do. I understand they did their best to help me, and they know not what they did. As they crossed two mountain ranges to get to our house, I knew there was time to kill. I readily agreed to the shower. In my sorely sleep-deprived and partially hallucinating brain, JD guided me into our bathroom. To me, he spoke and looked as if he were a tall, dark, and handsome, dark-eyed immortal. The shower would be, I believed, one of transformation, where I would gain immortality. But instead of something dark, like a vampire, I would become an earth angel, surpassing the need for physical death and joining my husband and those already crossed over in a secret crusade of helping others earn their wings. The test I had been required to pass to transform was my having endured the trauma of his betrayal and my willingness to stay and reconcile. In my mind, my parents already had transformed—to me, that was the explanation for their *"apparent"* inability to understand what was wrong with me. They were to take me away to a secret party where everyone who'd already crossed over would be waiting with open arms. Some of them had been guiding me and preparing me while playing other roles in my life, like a bizarre *Truman Show*, *The Sarah Show*. Maybe even Sr. Claire hadn't really died, and she'd be at the party. My goal was to get to the party, pass every test, and endure whatever was required until then.

I spent probably an hour in the special shower, letting water in my eyes, feeling like I was being resealed, even revirginized, in a waterfall-like rebirth. I had only ever had sex with JD as a human, and our next time would be spiritually intensified. I sat on the shower floor, my leg covering the drain, so it was as if a small pool had formed. While I meditated, the water comfortingly poured over my head. Eventually, I got out and put on my favorite pink robe, climbed into bed, and awaited my parents' arrival. I knew they would also help confirm that I was pregnant instead of being in my medically induced, totally out-of-it actual state. The three negative pregnancy tests meant nothing to me, and since JD still didn't believe that pee tests could be wrong, I believed a blood test was the next logical step. Deep down, I longed for a pregnancy that would make my life worth living, sanctifying me as a vessel for the unborn, and at the same time, it would surely keep us together.

My parents came to my bedside. Well, my dad saw me from the hallway, and my mom came in closer to see what was wrong. I probably told her I thought I was pregnant. But she probably saw something else in my glazed-over eyes and sleeplessness—that the prescriptions had run off with my former self. I made no sense, and I couldn't make sense. The ability to be logical escaped me. They knew the prescriptions I'd taken, and Sophie offered a cover story. She explained that a few rough court cases had taken their toll on me. I did have a couple of tough rulings, but I'd easily survived worse, things like losing my first trial or just taking the bar exam. How they so easily and without further question believed it was just work stress that brought me to oblivion is still beyond me. They were probably scared, too, and formulated a plan to get me into the hospital for a detox. They lied. They told me we would go to the ER for a pregnancy blood test to be administered. I trusted them. This sounded like a plan to me, and I rode with them while JD drove separately. Maybe he stayed behind to sleep a bit. I'm not sure.

The way my parents spoke to me in the car was calm and complacent, going along with whatever I said but not saying too much and not panicking. Everything they said, therefore, fit right in with my theory of crossing over to the immortal side. It even led me to question whether JD had already crossed or whether my breakdown was the thing he would endure to earn his stripes. When we got to the ER, I checked in and waited, having asked for the blood test. I later discovered that behind my back, my mom told them, as I later saw in my medical records, that I had a history of mania. She had diagnosed me as manic and gave her nurse's opinion to the ER staff and doctors as if it were true, as if it were an undisputed fact. My mom could be sneaky, sometimes slightly at my expense. This time was worse, but there was an earlier, minor infraction that could have clued me into a healthy distrust. We were at SeaTac airport, waiting for our flight to London for a month-long family holiday. Grandma had paid for the trip with an inheritance upon her fiftieth wedding anniversary, a bus tour that included Poland, which she wanted to see before she died. For her, it was the trip of a lifetime, a dream she made real. For us, a bit tortuous, but complaining was not an option because we hadn't paid. Waiting for the flight, my mom offered to share a cinnamon roll with me. She went to get it while I used the restroom. When I got to the gate, my half was waiting for me, the outer two rings of the roll. Her half was the inner, softest, and best-tasting part. My dad scolded her while I picked at the remains, and away we flew to London.

Waiting for the doctors in the halls of the ER, I thought, but never voiced that we were waiting for a secret party. When the party didn't seem to be happening soon, I tried bringing it to me. I said I was hungry. I wanted pizza. I would make it a pizza party. I was certain that just beyond the double doors at the end of the hall was the room full of people who loved me, people welcoming me to the other side since I'd so well survived my trials. I was interviewed by an intake person, and I left out the important part about learning about JD's cheating because my worst nightmare was my parents knowing. I remained scared their judgment would negatively affect my ability to reconcile with him. Or my ability to decide to reconcile with him. All I shared was that I felt fine until I got a bit stressed and then felt completely whacked out after taking a bunch of prescription drugs. Then I waited, waited, and waited. I made my family bring in pizza, and then, as they demolished it, I didn't even get one piece.

I went to the bathroom, pretended to break down crying, and waited for my mom and sometimes Jennah, who had also shown up, to come in and see what was wrong. Then I feigned feeling better, walked them back to the hospital bed I was waiting on, and had them sit up on it with me. In my fantasy reality, they would be allowed to accompany me to the party as my bed was wheeled through those double doors at the end of the hall, so I would do my best to figure out how to keep them on the bed with me. They unknowingly played along like puppets on strings, clueless that my scary behavior had a secret rhythm and meaning of its own.

I turned out to be the puppet. I kept desperately pleading, asking, begging my parents, "Can I have a sabbatical now?" *"No,"* they always responded. After asking probably dozens of times, I changed my tune. *"What will it take for you all to leave me alone???"* I asked, time after time after time. After hours of waiting, after pizza, after my being interviewed by staff, poked and prodded, hours more waiting, I finally was told what it would take for them to leave me alone: *"Sign here,"* they said.

I thought this was it! My ticket to freedom. Maybe to the party, if that really was what was going on. It was quiet like they were all hushed before shouting *surprise* as I entered. Next, the doors would open, and I'd be taken away. I signed. I even propped my legs up on the table, crossing them like a boss. So there!

But the surprise was, the doors were locked, and I was stuck inside and alone. Not free but abandoned. I had completely unknowingly and unwittingly signed myself into the mental ward.

Chapter 7

DIAGNOSIS: BIPOLAR

A skeleton night crew welcomed me to my new residence. I agreed to go straight to bed and took whatever pills they gave me. I assumed they would have the strength of a horse tranquilizer to put me out. They did. All I knew was that I didn't want to exist. I didn't know how to accept where I was. That the exit doors only opened one way. The reality was they put me away. Instead of waiting, instead of sitting on the bed with me at home and waiting for the truth. Did they have no bullshit radars? My dad judged people's veracity daily. It was his job. Why didn't they innately sense the story they were given didn't add up? Why didn't they push JD for more information? Why didn't they wait with me until I was finally honest (although I don't know how long that might have taken, given my fierce adversity to being vulnerable in their presence)? Why didn't JD give himself up? Same reasons as me, I suppose. I was taken away for inappropriate behavior, to be "helped" and made normal again. Kind of like when my dad sent our tree frogs away after my mom inappropriately caught a fly with her hand at a cocktail party in front of their friends. She was so used to feeding the frogs, but that act, in that setting, was intolerable for Dad. The next day, the tree frogs got a new home, and her fly-catching hand trap found other, more acceptable things to do. My behavior had to become normal again for me to be accepted. But they had no idea what I was dealing with or how my attempt at prescription drugs, a Western doctor's cure-all, had only made things worse.

In the morning, I discovered that my room was at least a room with a view. I could gaze down at the Port of Tacoma and see the building with the pyramid on top, where my thirteenth-floor office and client list awaited my return. In Italy, thirteen is a lucky number. I was surprised to find a building that honest about having a thirteenth floor, as so many of our buildings have one elevator that goes up 1-12 and the other 14 and up. Looking down on it now, it didn't feel so lucky. I couldn't remember the last work I'd done, certainly sometime before my brother's wedding. The big oval window was like a looking glass, and I was on the wrong side.

The dollhouse-like furniture in my room reminded me of my room in the pensione. I'd lived there during my junior year of college, when I'd spent nine months becoming fluent in Italian and painting frescoes at Gonzaga's campus in Florence, Italy. There was a wardrobe. There was a desk surface attached to the wall. The sink in the corner of the room had a mirror above it with an attached paper towel dispenser below. Only the toilet and shower were in the bathroom itself. The bed had wheels and a cord that was plugged into the wall so that it inflated back against the pressure of your body. I'm sure it was meant to be comfortable, but it bugged the crap out of me, and I had to unplug it to sleep. Yes, sleep! I was given more drugs that knocked me out. It was impossible to determine the time on the circular floor, as there were only a couple of wall clocks inside the nurses' station.

I was given no towel. I thought that was meant to be a challenge or test of some kind, like, *let's see if she figures this one out*. I used my T-shirt as a towel and wore my sweatshirt instead. I won that one! That was before I learned that, at the late hour I *"checked myself in,"* no one took the time to show me the linen closet with all the towels and cute scrubs I got to wear, with different colors flying across them like the falling spray of fireworks.

I soon found out that to get meals, I had to preorder during a certain pre-meal window of time. I'd missed that time since I didn't know the rules, and I tried to order a simple peanut butter and jelly sandwich. I was reverting to childhood for comfort—the only sandwich I ate in elementary school was peanut butter and jelly. Whenever I discovered a meat sandwich in my lunch bag when I got to school, I just went hungry. Like then, nothing but peanut butter and jelly sounded good. They said I couldn't order a sandwich in between meals. I asked if I could order bread. Peanut butter. And jelly. Yes, I could. Well, can I have all that then? Just when I'd made my sandwiches and organized a concert hall—using the movable furniture in the common area and the fish tank as the backdrop of the stage for the sad musician, whose best friend had just been killed in a car accident and he'd just begun playing his guitar for the first time since the accident—my family arrived with food. I abandoned my tray to take their bribe.

Before they arrived, I'd read in one of the common area magazines the factors that contribute to tubal pregnancies. I determined it could be that I had those factors, like the ones that caused my mom and sister to have irregular periods and potentially high-risk pregnancies. It also explained why the pee tests were negative. I was scared all the drugs I was being given were not only making me disintegrate mentally but also adversely affecting the potential pregnancy. I thought elevating the pregnancy to multiples would escalate the danger and lead to my being removed from that ward, where I could be further examined physically for abdominal pain. Instead, it just scared my parents. My mom said she would terminate such a high-risk pregnancy. My dad looked at me like I was an alien. I tried grabbing him and squeezing his hand or arm so hard that I scared him more instead of getting his complete attention or helping him see what was really going on. Their visit was ridiculous to me. I was so drugged I couldn't communicate. They wanted to see me *"normal,"* or at least on the road to normal. Instead, I was trapped and had no idea how to get myself out. They were of no use in that regard.

Later in the day, I noticed an older man hovering at the desk of the nurses' station while they shoved the menu in his face, asking him to order his dinner. I asked what was going on. They explained that for *"Fred"* to go home, he had to learn how to order his food. He reminded me of my grandpa. I remembered sitting on my grandpa's lap in the movie theater for my first movie, *E.T.* It was so crowded my brother sat somewhere else with Grandma. I imagined someone putting my grandpa through a similar trial soon, as he was near Fred's apparent age. It seemed to me like Fred was a widower, grieving while being forced to learn things his wife had obviously handled most of his adult life. I couldn't help but intervene.

I asked Fred if I could look at his menu. It was a huge menu, and it could have taken forever to go through it item by item with him. I had plenty of experience as a server at a golf course and a bar, so I took that angle. As the nurses looked on from behind their counter, I asked him, *"Fred, if you could have anything, what would you like for dinner?"* He said, *"A big juicy steak."* I cringed because that was not likely on our hospital food menu. I found some cut of beef that wasn't far off and broke the news I had something similar. Would he like it with vegetables, potato, and all the fixings? Oh yes! He smiled. *"Okay, I will make sure it's ready for you at dinnertime."* He hesitated, seeming confused. I asked him, *"What would you like to do now?"* He said he wanted to lie down. I gently pointed him in the direction of his room. Even for me, initially, our rooms weren't easy to find, with the ward being circular and all the doors looking alike. I knew easier from the window view which was which. I placed the menu on the nurses' counter, glared at them, and made them promise his dinner order would be placed. They were slightly in awe. It seemed to me like they had dissociated from what humane treatment might look like.

The menu was so thick because it had three parts, and three girls at the tables in the eating area were staring at it, confused about what to order because each section seemed just like the other. Again, I couldn't help them. I sat down and briefly shared that the first section was for people who want to lose weight. The middle section had food for people to maintain their weight, and the last section had foods that helped people gain weight. Then, I asked each of them what they wanted to do and pointed them toward the section that would help them accomplish their personal goals. They were ecstatic.

One girl was an overwhelmed new mom. She could have come right off the set of the MTV show *Teen Mom*, but I knew she wasn't a teenager. I liked her pink motorcycle hat and bartered with her to get it for myself. I drew under the brim in the blue pen a mountain scene to further make it *"mine"*because it then had my "art" on it.

One woman looked so sad I couldn't help but engage in conversation with her. Her long, graying hair was pulled back, revealing the sadness that permeated her eyes, face, and posture. I asked how she got here. She said, *"It was my husband's funeral. Police took me away from his gravesite after I broke down sobbing."* He had been her second husband, her second marital loss. Instead of being comforted, she was brought here to be fixed. She shared the story of her first husband with me, the love of her life, who had also died. As she shared, love welled up, and her eyes looked deeply into mine. I held eye contact with her as if breaking it would snap us out of the vulnerable share that we both were destined to participate in. She described him and their loving history. As I held her gaze, I swear his image, from his shoulders up, appeared in her eyes. I saw him. Then, almost like Whoopi's character in the movie *Ghost*, I told her he was there, and I hugged her for him. Next, she shared with me about her dead dog, who had been her favorite pet, and I saw him, too, in her eyes, looking attentively back at me, ears perked. Their images didn't freak me out at the time. It just seemed natural, like a previously invisible realm had been opened to me, and I had a new special talent.

I skipped all the *"group"* meetings. I only met with the psychiatrist, hoping it would lead to my release. I hoped to teach him a thing or two about how to treat people, as well, after what I'd witnessed. I had been repeatedly asked so many questions about whether I wanted to harm myself. When someone came to my room for a *"safety check,"* I asked what he was checking, as I was already staying in the room. He said he was looking for ways I could kill myself. Ah. *"Well, as I keep telling you, I'm not suicidal, but if I was, there are around a dozen ways. So, you can note down the curtains, the shower curtain, the cover on the paper towel holder has sharp edges, the cord from the bed, the screws in the handles, and hinges in the wardrobe..."* He scurried away in a hurry. Sick of the same questions, I asked the doctor why they don't just directly ask the patients why they are sad. What happened? What do they think would make them feel better now? I must have said it from a place of compassion because I saw a tear roll down his cheek. Still, he didn't ask me those questions. Instead, he diagnosed me with bipolar.

Five or six more prescriptions were administered as a cocktail. I was drugged to the moon upon arrival, and, in my opinion, more prescription drugs were supposed to bring me back into behaving like a *"monkey."* I was supposed to be grateful for the diagnosis and take all the medicine. I wonder, but doubt, if the doctor ever consulted my general practitioner, who worked in the women's clinic of the same hospital and originally got me started on prescription drugs. She was the one who knew and could have disclosed the trauma that triggered sleep deprivation and the countdown to meltdown. It was expected that I would start going to the support group. Instead, the new meds took me to a whole new level of whacked out.

I was also bored as fuck, having just come from working out seven days a week and running a law office while preparing for and standing up in three weddings in the prior four months. Now, I was a caged monkey with puzzles and books, crayons and paper, cutouts of animals, and Magic Markers. But the puzzles showed the result on the box—I was already bored. The book covers were giveaways and already bored me. I came up with ways to entertain myself, like pasting the animal cutouts all over the stark white walls and across the tables. That was a fun game until the nurses began to utter admonishment, and I'd just as quickly clear them all away. Then, there was the drink-mixing game. There wasn't exactly much variety in the way of beverages in a hospital mental ward so I took to using the three to four typical options of apple, cranberry, orange, and maybe grape to make a greater selection. I proudly shared with the pasty white, plainly attired nurses some of my delicious work, explaining that I held a Class 13 Mixologist permit. In Washington state, that meant I was legal to serve and mix alcoholic beverages, something that was required when I was a cocktail server at the W Hotel during law school. To my dismay, I discovered later that this was recorded in my medical records as *"she says she's a scientist."* Seriously. But also, how does one challenge the content of medical records?

I wanted to call Sophie to get her help to get out. I once got her on the phone, and she had no idea what I was saying as I talked a hundred miles a minute, but just hearing her voice made me feel better. Then, I was denied phone access other than to the kitchen to order food according to the special schedule. I asked for my cell phone because I hadn't memorized Sophie's number anyway.

Denied. In the outside world, I had a lot to do. I was worried about the cases that were probably being continued or just being passed off. I was still concerned about the outcomes and the care of the clients whose fate I used to competently handle from across the sky on the thirteenth floor of the pyramid-topped building, staring back at me just out my window. Frustrated and messed up by even more meds, I began to reference Sophie as *"Red,"* as if I needed a red phone to dial her the way Reagan could dial Russia during the Cold War. My life *was* officially in a kind of war status, and no one was at the other end of the line for me. Last year, Sophie jokingly gave me a piggy bank in the shape of a red phone. I wish I didn't remember that part of things, but I do. I'm sure it will be funny to me someday, too, but it's still too soon.

When I was unable to access Sophie or get any medical attention for the side effects of my hair falling out in clumps or the ongoing abdominal pains, I came up with a way that I thought I could permanently seal my medical records. I thought I could own the experience by transforming it into art, my art, that the hospital would have no right to retain or record. I think I even asked my brother about the laws regarding intellectual property and art because he has a Master of Laws in intellectual property. He probably had no idea where that was coming from. I *"reasoned"* that if there were things I was asked to sign by drawing pictures everywhere across my records, they couldn't even keep them in my medical records. I became an artist. I made everything into art so that I would own it. I tied the curtains into sculpture-like roses and lion's heads. I found a brochure with a black man's face on it that resembled JD's. I drew JD's face on the brochure, made him look like a devil, and, after getting home, even posted the sketch on a blog page. He, of course, got upset, and I agreed to take it down. I drew on the floor and wall in the bathroom, though my drawings were easily cleaned off. I drew on T-shirts. I drew on the inside of my cargo pants, thinking it would be a great maternity design. How cute would it be to have expectant mothers place pictures of what they wanted to teach their children against their bellies while they waited for their child to arrive? I flipped through magazines and drew with Sharpies across the ads I saw on the covers, morphing them into more art. I was entertaining myself in my totally drugged-out state. The new meds had put me into a worse tailspin than the original partygoers.

Also, I still needed to find a way home. They told me I wasn't pregnant, but I read an article in one of the magazines about endometriosis and polycystic ovary disease. I knew my mom and sister were polycystic, and I was certain I must have both, and that was why I had the abdominal pain. Maybe it was a tubal pregnancy. I wanted an ultrasound because the pain was worsening. I said that if I had a high-risk pregnancy near a tube or somehow attached somewhere outside the uterus, I would keep the baby/babies. My mom said she would have such a pregnancy terminated. She would kill my babies. It wasn't even a sure or likely scenario—a pregnancy had yet to be detected—but she was serious. She would kill my baby to save her baby. I was floored that she even felt she decided to make it and more scared that she would do what it took to make that decision for me. I believed an unusual and hard-to-detect pregnancy would explain my abdominal pain, and my wanting to not harm an unborn child with the meds I was put on was more reason for me to fight to get out, get home, and get med-free.

I gave it my all. I played along and took the pills. I suffered through the visits with my family. I'd originally tried getting through to them, but it didn't work anyway. At one point, I told my dad I was sick of him telling me I was stupid. Shocked, he said he'd never done that. I said yes, he did, with all the dumb blonde jokes over the years. He paused and apologized, but his apology seemed less sincere and more delivered to tame me. I was so pissed off at them for tricking me into being there and for so easily believing that I was suddenly bipolar. I remember how I failed to get through to him and got so frustrated that I grabbed his arm to get him into my reality physically. I wanted to somehow shock him into a place where he could finally listen. Instead, I scared him. I saw the fear instead of understanding in his eyes, and I gave up. I was resigned to feeling like I had been drugged into a parallel universe where understanding and being understood were not possible. They would not help me, so I had to find a way to help myself.

Eventually, I threatened to sue the shit out of the hospital for not diagnosing the cause of the abdominal pains, the hair falling out, my skin irritations, etc. Eventually, I think both the hospital and JD couldn't take it anymore, and the hospital agreed to sign me out to his care, even though I was technically leaving against medical advice. A timid male nurse came in to give me my last dose of prescriptions, saying I could leave if I took them all. Down the hatch, and I was free.

Chapter 8

FREEDOM WAS FLEETING

At St. Joseph's, I took the pills they required for me to then leave the hospital against medical advice. I'm sure JD was scared, but he signed off on letting me come home. My wedding rings were returned to me, but I hesitated to put them back on my finger. I don't remember the short drive home, but almost as soon as I got through the front door, I suffered a fresh batch of side effects, and nothing at home felt right. Nothing was resolved.

I felt safest talking to someone who was required to keep everything in confidence because I knew on some level how bizarre my experiences were, but I was also still afraid for my real problems to be out in the open. I wanted support in secret. Lawyers and priests are bound by confidentiality. I made an appointment with Father Dan.

I walked into the church office, a small room in a manufactured building on the church's campus. The church itself and its copper dome and large carved wooden doors stood protectively nearby. I waited while the receptionist made sure he was aware that I had arrived. I felt I was on a sacred mission. The setup of the church offices and the infrastructure of the church itself was the perfect way for the chosen immortals to communicate with one another. I wouldn't be let in on it openly until I'd completed all my tasks, but the people with lighter eyes than normal were the ones I could trust. And Father Dan had bright, light blue eyes.

We sat opposite each other in a small, plainly decorated meeting room. I felt safe sharing my situation. I started with the cheating, which led to the prescriptions and the hospitalization. I asked if he got the envelope, and he said he did, but that I didn't need to worry about it as it was just political notes and not important. I thought that was code, for he had passed it along to the right people. Then, without sharing the immortality theory, I instead shared about the dead people reaching out to me, how I saw the husband and dog in the woman's eyes, and the original Do Not Be Afraid experience in Italy. Father Dan made those things seem normal. He comfortingly said something like some people are more sensitive to seeing things like that than others, and often, others don't understand it. He said I should keep these visions to myself but continue being open to them. He said the ability to see them sometimes runs in families, which further confirmed my theory about my brother's untapped potential. He also encouraged me just to be a wife. Don't worry about work or anything else; just be a wife, and everything else will fall into place. This advice just reaffirmed my inability to consider leaving JD. The sacramental bond of marriage had become excruciating bindings. Because of my faith, I felt irrevocably tied to him in marriage. Instead of considering leaving him, I gave way to the decision being made for me. I was going to stay and let it all come around, like Father Dan said was possible.

As I suffered new side effects from all those new meds, and despite Father Dan's advice, JD and I began to fight.

The hospitalization had been like putting me into a pressure cooker, and my release allowed me to explode finally. I was admittedly and desperately out of control. I was dramatic and extreme, desperate for my reality to be as it was before the Last Supper. But that, of course, was not an option, and JD's automatic and fear-driven response was to exert as much force toward controlling me as possible. He kept me in the house and kept me from my phone, away from any access to the internet or the ability to communicate with the outside world. To protect me, and maybe partly to protect himself, from exposure of his transgression. But that was a double-edged sword, as while I couldn't damage any client relationships or pending cases, I also couldn't reach out for support.

It felt like there was no way to get through to him. I was so frustrated, and to get his attention, I slammed my favorite pink insulated water bottle onto the hardwood black coffee table, accidentally shattering it and scaring the shit out of him at the same time. A shard of the coffee table had flown just past his head. I was officially uncontrollable, and he must have felt as helpless as I had once I discovered I was stuck in a mental ward.

To test him, I made him re-propose to me. I wanted some control and to hear his desire to commit to the vows that, deep down, I felt he still couldn't honor. At the time, I didn't understand why. He had said all the right things for years, but on another level, he had his own issues, and I had become collateral damage. I didn't realize before how deeply his childhood affected him. His father basically exiled his mother from Haiti after she gave birth to a son and was done nursing him. JD and his sister Lucy stayed behind to be raised by the servants and Christian missionary caretakers who were more present in their lives than their father, a hellfire-and-damnation-preaching Baptist minister. I often heard JD refer to him as the "Billy Graham of Haiti," who in those days, ran his house like a dictator and devoted most of his life to prayer and preaching. The marriage was probably arranged, I assumed, because his middle-aged father desired a son to take over his church in the future. First, came a girl; then, upon his son's birth, he sent their mother to live in the US. His mother's pseudo-banishment was like abandonment for him. How could this not have affected his ability to be in and maintain intimate, long-term relationships? Maybe underneath, he only felt worthy of more abandonment and didn't feel worthy of lifelong, unconditional love. Maybe he sabotaged our relationship. Even in JD's baby photos, he's plump, chubby, and happy until she's gone. Then he becomes gaunt, thin, with big, sad eyes. A little boy who needed his mom.

At one point, he broke down into tears, a husband in need of his wife. But because of the meds, I was way behind the curve. The ability to face and process the trauma of his broken vows was not in my bag of tricks. I had nothing when it came to coping with personal trauma. My abilities were finely tuned in helping friends and fighting for others in court. I was at a total loss. Instead of fight or flight, I was suffering a complete meltdown. I later learned it's called adjustment disorder in the DSM, the handbook of definitions that allows psychiatrists to bill insurance companies. Because of the side effects and because I was finally losing it, I just couldn't behave normally. I still couldn't sleep, and overnight, I trashed the house in my dreamlike state to demonstrate to the viewer (I expected it to be my family) how they had helped to destroy me and my marriage. I wrote on the countertop and the mirrors in Sharpie. I photographed my favorite things to remember them like a photo museum of a life once lived and still longed for. I tried making sense, still reaching for a logical explanation for my behavior. Did the hormones of a bizarre pregnancy influence it? Although theoretically possible, my sole coping skill of rationalizing was not serving me well at all. Of course, none of it made sense to JD. He was scared and couldn't *"control"* me, and the water bottle was the last straw. He called 9-1-1. I was removed from the house with an ambulance as my chariot.

Chapter 9

SHOT AFTER A FAILED GANDHI-LIKE ESCAPE ATTEMPT

I expected another stint at the hospital, which I knew I could survive. I needed space from JD anyway. Instead, the men in blue took me someplace called Recovery Innovations. It was a kind of holding facility located near the state mental hospital. I'm still not sure how they could hold me against my will without any kind of hearing or court order. Maybe it was a weekend, but there I was, and they drugged me worse than I'd ever been drugged before. To me, this place had nothing to do with recovery but plenty to do with torture.

Once inside, there was no way out. All exit doors were locked. The entry, if it had signage, might as well have said, *"Give up hope, all ye who enter."* It looked more like the gate I'd seen at the concentration camp Dachau years ago. I pushed and pushed and pushed against the door with a metal handle that, instead of letting me out, barred me in. The facility's layout was a lot like my elementary school, with two options at either end of a long hall. But instead of classrooms, either side of the hall had cells for us inmates. At one end, the staff offices were opposite the community room where food was served, and activities could be done at the other, like childhood games, cards, crayons, markers, pictures to color, what you would have expected to see at a primary school. The staff didn't wear uniforms, and what I found most bizarre was that time spent talking to someone left me thinking they were a fellow inmate when it turned out they were staff. Sometimes, the staff members were more depressed than those of us being medicated.

All I wanted was air, free, fresh air, and a chance to run away. I was fast; I expected to make it quite far if not all the way to safety, if I got the chance. The others got to have air during smoke breaks, but I didn't smoke, so I said I did. Then I tried to be part of the group that got air breaks, but I wasn't allowed. I sat against the exit door. Which I still couldn't open. Locked in. Stuck. Nothing to do. I waited, hoping someone on the other side might need in, might give me the window I needed.

I refused the meds, of course, and demanded JD be there to give them to me himself. Partly to torture him as much as I was being tortured, but more to begin saving myself. The pills here were the kind that dissolves in your mouth, probably to make it so that you can't hide them and spit them out. I would have him give them to me from his mouth to mine, and I poured liquid for swallowing them in between our mouths, letting them dissolve into the floor instead of in my mouth to avoid taking them. Sometimes, a faint color of what was supposed to be down my throat would be against the side of the pillow, so I flipped it over when he left.

I wanted me back, too, but somewhere deep inside, I knew that prescription drugs were not my ruby red slippers.

Time was impossible to track, and the more I came out of it, the more it seemed my best way out was to stay close to the exit itself. I picked one end of the hall, the door that opened more often and sat on the floor against the door. I was desperate to escape, not just the facility but my life, and getting out of this prison block was step one. When some staff asked me nicely to move, I tried negotiating for a phone call, to no avail. They wouldn't offer anything in return for my compliance; they just kept demanding I move. In my still sleep-deprived, dreamlike mind, I tried controlling what seemed like a dream from inside my head. I told myself this must be a test.

A year ago, I applied to be in the Jesuit Volunteer Corps, and this whole experience is a test where I pass and get into the corps if I behave properly, reacting peacefully instead of resorting to violence. Then, they tried to lift me up and away physically. I just sat, making myself dead weight. Suddenly, and before I knew what was going on, four of them—four of them—grabbed me. Two on either side. I couldn't keep myself down. There were two on each arm. Four hands on each arm. A fifth, who I had asked to simply make a phone call in exchange for moving, a guy with curly brown hair and glasses like Waldo, stood aside, just witnessing. I flashed back to the time I lived in Australia and a guy had taken me into an alley outside a club and wouldn't let me go when I refused to do more than kiss him, and my gut turned inside out. He had grabbed my arms, and my only way to free myself had been to twist my wrists out and down, but he grabbed me again, harder the second time. He grabbed me a third time before two guys bigger than him walked by, and he got distracted and let me go. I like to believe those two bigger guys were angels in disguise. At least, they were to me.

Instinctually, and with that flashback whiting out my ability to think, I twisted my arms around and down to free myself of the four-person grasp. I was standing and had good leverage. All easily let go but one. One, a woman with short, straight brownish hair and sharply defined facial features, resisted my movement. She grabbed me back so hard, so tight that the friction instantly burned. When I later got home, I discovered I had a series of bruises on my upper right arm in the shape of her fingers. As soon as I stood, after I thought the situation had been diffused, the shortest one who had run off ran back at me and, without warning, gave me a shot in my left arm. There was nothing I could do to avoid the shot that I didn't see coming.

I have no idea what it was, but to me, it was some form of poison—and I didn't even get the dignity of it having been disguised in a shiny red apple. Everything went dark.

JD had to fill in the blackness for me later. He said that I apparently then stood in a corner of that hallway for over eight straight hours, not moving. Not speaking. Not existing, except in far-off, drug-induced oblivion.

I don't know when, but I also hallucinated the strangest things. I remember sitting on the bed of my cell, which looked like something a nun in a convent valuing poverty would inhabit. The lights were off, except the door was cracked because they checked on you every hour or more, and it caused a bright light to reflect off the floor and travel up the side of the wall. After staring at the light long enough, it began to shimmer and appeared to rise like an upside-down fountain of gold. I believed it was a bird's-eye view of all the souls who had died in the earthquake in Haiti rising from their deaths into heaven.

I had dreams unlike any other. One was about the sequel to the last *Twilight* movie, where I was Bella. She's been isolated into the same kind of ward where I was being held, and it turns out to have served as the method for her escape. Once the humans thought she was done for, she finally pushed against that exit door to find Edward on the other side. It was her time to join them in an infinite lifetime of freedom, good works, and happiness. I woke up ready to write it and hoping the original author would approve. Mostly, that shot caused me to have dreams that tortured me. They were dreams of my worst nightmares, and my deepest fears came true before I learned from a clown (which might have been me unknowingly talking to one of my fellow convicts) that they weren't true. First, that I'd been molested as a child, like raped, but by who? Second, that I'd been raped in Australia one night after drinking too much while I was an exchange student. But then the clown whispered to me that none of it was true.

Was my breakdown, in part, a delayed reaction or some PTSD from these horrible past traumas? No, not really. That was a nightmare-induced rationalization and the refusal to face that I was suffering from current trauma from a husband I felt like I couldn't escape. Because of should. Because of Catholicism. Because I'd have to share with the world that my husband cheated on me, so what was wrong with me? Because then my marriage failed, so what was wrong with me? Did it mean I had made the wrong choice, chosen the wrong man to give all of myself to for all my days? Did, according to Catholic teaching, I form an unbreakable bond with a man who had no ongoing intention of living the vows that I took seriously? I was cut to my core.

The clown reassured me those things didn't happen, but I was fearful they might have. I worried I was one of those people who buried childhood traumas, which led to me having even more twisted, dreamlike hallucinatory suspicions. Things related to the church and how it secretly selected certain young people to use for its bidding. That one could almost be the basis of an entire fiction series, where the secretly selected youth were, like Bella in my version of *Twilight*, carefully extracted from their lives for use or training for certain missions. Sometimes, they were even used for breeding, where certain girls' bodies were manipulated into serving as incubators for litters of special humans. I was really cracking up. I almost mentally gave in to the bipolar diagnosis at that point.

Still, I truly believed that my peaceful protest against the door would lead to my freedom. I held the secret hope that my tolerating the abuse was a sort of test. Like, if I passed this ultimate test of inhumane treatment, I'd be accepted into a secret society— even if not the JVC. It was, and remains, impossible for me to accept that what was happening to me was right in any way, shape, or form. Because it wasn't. The place was a mini prison. I still don't know how I was able to be held.

I had to come up with a new plan of escape, as the door, ironically, wasn't the way out. I complained more aggressively about my ongoing abdominal pain. I was ignored. I don't even know if the complaint made my chart. The staff people have so messed up themselves I still couldn't tell who worked there versus who was a fellow inmate. When my complaints of severe stomach pain made no headway, I designed a Plan C.

I behaved. I learned who the staff were and became all *"buddy-buddy"* with them. They allowed patients to roam their offices a bit, so this gained me access to the room with desks and phones. This time JD had refused to sign me out like he had days ago at the hospital. He refused to have a hand in my leaving that inferno.

As soon as no one was paying much attention, I quickly snatched up a phone and, as fast as possible, dialed 9-1-1. No one was looking. I made the call! But the operator said I wasn't allowed to call from where I was. As if 9-1-1 had already *"helped"* me and there was nothing for them to do. I've never been good at taking no, and I persisted in telling her about my severe abdominal pain, for which they were doing nothing. I begged and pleaded for her to help me get the ability (and, subsequently, freedom) to have it evaluated in an ER. Finally, a victory. One for my W column. I left that prison in yet another ambulance ride, JD driving behind my chariot in his two-door Honda. We'd bought it from my dad as a low-maintenance, low-cost commuter. It still had the Christian radio, American flag, and Rotary Club stickers on it, but he had personalized its license plate to read LFTSEAT. The left seat in the cockpit is the captain's seat. He was all about being captain, being the boss, and being in control of everything. He was most secure with a chain of command at the top. Now I realize the

Honda was never good enough for him. To me, he was hardly home enough to make it worth a second luxury car payment. And anyway, he had readily agreed to the first one he now complained about, preferring a car payment to the maintenance costs of my beloved '96 BMW 328is.

At St. Claire's, I was evaluated for abdominal pain, and they found nothing. But because they did no ultrasound and laid no hands on me for any real physical exam, I still questioned its source and cause. Because I had come from a special facility to the ER, a mental health professional had to evaluate me before I could finally be freed. The MHP was an older, gray-haired man with glasses, Grandpa's age. His brow and face were furrowed with strict, judgmental scrutiny as he interviewed me. Without hesitation, I threatened to sue the shit out of Recovery Innovations, showing him the bruising on my upper right arm. I told him about the misdiagnosis of the St. Joseph's hospital psychiatrist, who reported I was suddenly bipolar and threatened to sue the pants off his ass too.

It wasn't long before it seemed he recognized which doctor I was talking about. He seemed to become a little intimidated by me, except his reaction was to threaten me right back. He said to JD and I, *"I will let you go this time, but if I ever see your face again, I'll make sure you get locked up."* He strongly recommended I go to a faraway county and sign myself in somewhere for a few weeks.

There was, of course, zero chance of that happening, but I was finally homeward bound. I made my own freaking ruby red slippers.

Chapter 10

NOW WHAT?

JD soon went back to work, which had become his escape. The home was no longer where he got support and comfort but the reverse. He left me in the care of my mom, who had agreed to medicate me with the half dozen prescriptions I was given for bipolar. She sat at the kitchen table in my usual seat and where I had sat the night of the Last Supper. Her mere presence agitated me because, to me, she believed the diagnosis, and her main role was not to comfort me but to medicate me. Another nurse was doing what she believed was right. I had to get rid of her. Get her out of my house, out of my life. Threats had worked at the hospital, so they were my go-to.

When I told her to go, she just sat there, unmoving and hardly engaging with me. I reminded her of her *"momma bear"* mode. It's what Dad calls those times that she goes nuts and would do anything to protect us, kids. I created an exponentially more threatening monster. *"You are threatening me and my family, and I'm not just 'momma bear,' I am a seven-headed, fire-breathing dragon and will destroy you if you don't get out of my house!"* I was practically screaming. If I really had breath of fire, she would no longer be with us. Her eyes glazed over, and she stared at me more blankly than before. Eventually, she relented. She didn't try talking to me, possibly afraid to make me worse. She didn't hug me. She finally left. Maybe she realized she was doing me no good.

I still thought I might have a rare type of pregnancy and my potential child/children to protect. My mom had already told me she would terminate a high-risk pregnancy over my objections, which were based on the uber-Catholic values they raised me with. The amount of biology I'd learned in undergrad was working against me because, despite all the negative test results, I knew either a tubal or rarer abdominal pregnancy could still be possible. I couldn't think of any other reason for my abdominal pains. As soon as Mom left, I flushed all the pills. I planned to detox myself. I went to an acupuncturist. I got a therapist. I started martial arts classes to learn how to kill people. No one would bruise me again.

I went to acupuncture a couple of times, desperate to cleanse myself. To detox myself from the inside out and be free of the meds' effects on me. I wanted to be me again. I know that's what everyone else wanted, too, but none of us, for whatever reason, knew what that was. My family still believed in prescriptions, if not that I was bipolar. I told JD I would only stay with him where I was drug-free. I drew a line in the sand. My breakdown kicked us off the road to reconciliation, leaving us in a limbo of sorts because things became about me getting better. How could I, though, without a resolution between us? It was a vicious circle. Keeping his betrayal a secret kept my parents out of our marriage, but, in a sick twist of fate, it had led to their betraying me by tricking me into signing myself in.

I just longed for freedom. But true freedom would come at the expense of more than I realized. I would have to lose it all to regain myself. Not just lose it all but be betrayed by my inner circle. Betrayal and loss became the crosses I bore. All while I was allegedly, suddenly permanently crazy, bipolar for life.

Meanwhile, JD escaped judgment. I deteriorated to protect him and what we no longer had—and maybe never really did. Or, if we did, it was a moment in a lifetime instead of the lifelong love I dreamt of. That was harder to swallow than any pill.

I had always dreamt of a love that could survive anything. I thought that's what we had. For a while, we survived a long-distance relationship because of his job flying. We overcame the difference in our Catholic and Baptist faiths, the difference in our colors, in our backgrounds. I believed all of it made us stronger. I wanted to continue believing that. I couldn't accept that I had made a mistake choosing him. How could I accept that it was a mirage? The façade was as unreal and shallow as any church's marble façade in Italy, covering a vast sea of plain, ugly red bricks. I was too naïve to realize sooner. Too inexperienced in life. Too attached to my sheltered and limited, rose-colored view of the world. And I totally lost myself in the *"shoulds"* and expectations of others.

I lost the ability to hear, let alone trust my gut. But through the torture, my gut made a comeback. First, I knew without a doubt after the wreckage that started with Valium that meds were not the way. And I knew that I wasn't bipolar. It wasn't like my entire life had been a little unstable, and this diagnosis made so much sense. For a while, though, a small part of me was scared that it was true. Not only would I then be coping with a cheating spouse and parents I no longer trusted, but I would also be working out how to overcome being bipolar. I held the possibility that I could be but knew I wasn't at the same time. I later got the correct diagnosis: adjustment disorder. It is a temporary breakdown in the face of extreme trauma, from which one fully and naturally recovers after the trauma subsides. Well, I was married to my trauma. Could I recover until JD was out of the picture? I didn't think I had any other option; a sacramental marriage was to the death.

I got a therapist, Kari. She is also a licensed attorney. I figured she would, therefore, understand the stress level I was dealing with and how to work toward a resolution with my judge father. It felt like my job was just to get better, going to therapy three times a week, acupuncture, and martial arts lessons in the evenings. But I couldn't seem to get better fast enough for JD. Whenever he was home, things felt a little bit worse, not better.

We had one getaway weekend at Orcas Island. I was going, I declared, and he was welcome to join me. We took Teddy. We rode the ferry toward the unknown, a place he hadn't been before. He always complained that he'd never traveled around Washington or that we hadn't been to Jazz Alley. But he also hadn't wanted to spend the money. I didn't know that he'd been spending so much on the road. As the "captain," he was expected to be the man to pick up the tab, and it was happening all too often. JD always stayed in hotels on the road and typically turned down the chance when he was home, and I wanted a getaway because he just wanted to be home. But he wanted the home to be kept like a hotel, perfectly clean. He was used to living in hotels with maid service or, as a kid, with servants. Sometimes, he'd stayed temporarily at crash pads. Still, even those were run kind of like hostels and typically clean because everyone had sparse belongings, only the things that fit into their black, wheeled pilot suitcases.

We got to our hotel on the island, and it was the last good time we had together. I tested him, expressing an interest in art to see if he would accept me with a new identity as a potential artist or anything other than a lawyer. I tested him further, proposing one night after a few drinks that he think about becoming the next president of Haiti if he really wanted to make a difference down there. Because of his dad's history, I wondered if it was an actual possibility. He had been sad since the prior January when we took our last vacation to Florence in the aftermath of the disastrous earthquake. JD played along, and we talked more than usual, but about nothing of substance, of the cheating, or the reality of what might be next. We shared a bath as we had the morning after our wedding and had bone-crushingly amazing, almost spiritual, sex. It was like a Hail Mary effort to get on the path to reconciliation that really wasn't destined to happen.

Sometime after that weekend and with JD back at work again, I tried getting an ultrasound at Virginia Mason, where my heart was fixed, and I got the anointing of the sick beforehand from the priest who'd advised, post-cheating, to focus on being a wife first and not worry about work, etc.

I took my sister with me so that she could drive. I still felt off from all the prescriptions. When my sister took me to Virginia Mason for the ultrasound, my brother showed up. He announced himself as my lawyer but said that I needed to be committed. I was stunned. I called a friend, a lawyer I had worked with before and whose work I admired. Mike came to my rescue. In superhero fashion, he took my call like a *"Mike signal"* and got to the hospital from Tacoma in record time. He was still in a gray suit and light-colored shirt, his take on a hero's costume, which he would automatically and humbly deny. His hair was slightly disheveled, as it was near the end of the day, and his glasses slightly lowered on his nose as he dashed through the door to assess the situation. He did not hesitate to act on my behalf. His mere presence calmed me.

Finally, someone was on my side. Team Sarah just grew by one. I was panicky, scared to death of my family's wish to commit me coming true. He was reassuring and met with me in private, coaching me as if he were a live Idiot's Guide to *"how to pass an interview with an MHP (mental health professional)."* I'd gotten past my first one at St. Claire's, but I didn't think threatening to sue the shit out of everyone was an MO that could be applied with success in every such interview. It felt like my family, waiting in the hall and then the waiting room, was out there saying:

Commit her!
Commit her!!
Commit her!!!

Without Mike to advise me and broker a resolution with my family, I shudder to think what might have otherwise happened that day. The ultrasound was complete, Mike arranged to give me a ride to a friend's house, and my family would drop my Infiniti at my house the next day. Away we drove, as I tried acting more myself alone with him in the car. I'm sure he offered consolation and additional advice besides a ride. It was excruciatingly embarrassing to have someone from the legal community aware of my situation, but it was equally reassuring that he was bound from publicity by confidentiality.

Mike left me at my friend's house, but I was feeling humiliated by the whole situation. I woke up at like 4 or 5 a.m., out of sorts, and asked her just to bring me home. I was mortified she had to be involved. My family had kept my car from me, and they dropped it off the next day. I soon got the results back, negative. The pregnancy, no matter how bizarre, that I had both feared and hoped for did not exist.

I could finally put that issue to rest. Still, in a way, believing in it had gotten me home. There was 100% no chance I had an abdominal pregnancy. My ability to intellectualize had, to some extent, gotten the best of me, but I had been totally overmedicated and grasping at straws by that point. I even emailed the OB-GYN in Canada, who I'd been talking to because he'd handled an abdominal pregnancy, to tell him mine was a *"false alarm."*

It was my therapist, Kari, who helped me get real. She didn't mess around and put me to work. I got homework. Kari had me physically print out the side effects of each of the dozen or so prescriptions I was given before and during my stays at St. Joseph's and Recovery Innovations. She told me to highlight all the side effects I'd experienced from each one. Ta-da. The number one side effect was abdominal pain, of course, and hallucinations, confusion, and many others were included. Those things were happening, and it was simply related to the meds. However, I still wondered what my disintegration could be related to—bipolar? She sent me for an evaluation by a psychiatrist she regularly worked with, Dr. M. He heard the whole story and sat with both JD and me to tell us that he felt the adjustment disorder was more in line with what had occurred. I was to guard my sleep and wait and see seriously. He wasn't very detailed about recovery, but I was working with Kari, and I googled more about it. He agreed I should stay prescription-free and was adamant about sleep.

From the beginning, Kari recommended I not work for six months. After I got home, I also went back to my office. I quickly lost Sophie, my only assistant. She kept the doors open while I was MIA, but the drama of my mess was too much. She was done. Luckily, she did everything right by calling the bar ethics hotline for guidance while I was trapped in the tower of St. Joseph's mental ward and then worse. She had originally intended to work for me for six months, and that had turned into over a year.

I needed someone nice to take the calls and hang out with me while I did what I knew deep down would be best: close shop. So, I hired Tyler, the tattooed whiz kid from Walmart, and he agreed to double his income and help me out. I wrapped things up and officially closed in December. That year, I sent no office Christmas cards. It was all over. Besides the office, I had to take an indefinite leave from Tacoma 8 Rotary and quit Fircrest Golf Club, as well, because the office income had supported those memberships. By December, I was totally adrift from my former life. The furniture and equipment that didn't fit at home I moved to temporary storage without knowing how long I could afford that.

Quitting felt like the right thing to do, especially according to the TV test that my former law partner had taught me. If this played out on TV, how would people respond? If I continued to practice with the shadow of instability—with a bipolar diagnosis hanging over me—would all my work be questioned? Would I potentially harm clients? Would it subject me to malpractice claims? Whether I could handle it or not, I thought it just didn't look good, either from a distance or up close. Plus, even though I didn't accept the diagnosis and believed I was capable of practicing, I wasn't feeling it. I couldn't bear mistakes like having mistakenly chosen the wrong guy to marry or having mistakenly chosen to keep my office open to the public. As a small girl, maybe around six, I used to take ballet and tap dance lessons. I hated the tights and leotards, but I loved ballet. I also hated that in tap class, but especially in performances, everyone could not only see but hear your mistakes. Your foot made noise when it shouldn't have. That mortified me. Because I was expected to be the best. Perfection was hard to fake in tap. I asked to quit tap class, but they said ballet and tap were required to be taken together. I couldn't take one without the other. I quit both.

At home, I was surrounded by the things we acquired from our wedding and my former law office. Around town, I mainly stuck to the grocery store and YMCA. Without my office and the rest of my former activities, going into Tacoma felt like I was haunting the carcass of my past life. The bony remnants scattered around the house.

JD was all about money, and what would I do now to make mine? I kept claiming I was *"wicked smart"* when I was messed up from the meds. He kept saying, *"Where is that smartness now?"* Like I wasn't allowed a temporary mental disability, like the in-sickness-and-health part of the vows was optional.

Around the same time as closing my law office, I considered selling purses and scarves from Italy. I even made business cards and laid out some *"samples"* in my spare office, as if testing the waters for how it might feel. No passion followed, and I let go of that idea, too. I considered being a designer with a friend and buying a condo in Tacoma that would be our studio. It would also be a place where I could live away from JD like I could go away to my place every month while he goes away… While it was fun to dream up options, even though nothing panned out, nothing could bring me a feeling of satisfaction. What I really wanted was to work things out with JD, and that's what the universe gave me: more wanting.

Chapter 11

A LAWYER TURNED CAR SALESMAN

JD was home that Christmas, but I was disengaged during all our time together. Disassociated with life, with feeling, and especially with the alleged diagnosis. I was just trying to cope with myself. JD attended counseling sessions with me at times, but they were my sessions. We only went to a few *"us"* sessions with a separate marriage counselor. I had become the focus, and it seemed like until my health was better, there was nothing left for us to work on.

It was early February 2011 when I found the job posting on Craigslist. Around that time, JD had come home and informed me that if I didn't go back to work, he'd leave me. I had been taking my therapist's advice to not work for six months. I'd just learned that my grandma had been diagnosed with terminal cancer and had only a few months to live. My grandma was more like a second mother to me. She was my mom's mother, and as far back as I can remember always lived across town, never more than about a five-minute drive from our house. Even when we moved across the river, she and Papa did, too. Grandma was at every ball game every band and choir performance. Papa was right beside her. He worked as a janitor at the local department store.

Still, he had also been Army police in WWII and then campus security for the University of Illinois before they left Chicago for Washington State. He was less vocal, mostly watching fights on television or cracking jokes around the table when he wasn't dodging her honey-do list. She cheered loudest in the stands for us and was there whenever Mom or Dad weren't, for rides, for sleepovers, for listening and advice. She was the youngest of ten kids and had worked as an assistant in an optometrist's office. She had seen it all when it came to people's behavior. Her advice was always the best. The thing I never understood, though, was how she didn't challenge Mom or Dad when they'd frequently tell her she was flat wrong about things—all kinds of topics and family history—even when they were the ones in the wrong. I did get to ask her about that when I was struggling to challenge them and their conviction in my bipolar diagnosis. She explained she was always afraid that my parents would distance us kids from her if she did, and she was more interested in keeping the peace and letting it all go. Preserving the family. Since my mom was an only child and it was always just the seven of us, I can understand her feeling that way. I desperately wanted to visit her, not commit my days to a new job, but JD was firm.

Neither my grandmother's, nor my uncertain condition seemed to affect JD's perception of what was necessary. Looking back, I wonder if it could have been a lawyer advising him that it would be better for him if I were working when he divorced me so he could avoid paying spousal support. Whether that really was behind it, I'll never know. Waiting the full six months in accordance with my therapist's recommendation would have meant going back to work in April, but at that point, I reacted as expected to his threat. When I got home in the fall and decided to close my law office, we had stopped making payments on the house, and some other bills, and it was wearing on him mentally. Because I'd been hospitalized, we had experienced a "hardship" in our household, and I knew we would easily qualify to get a modification of our home loan, but that didn't matter or register with him. He did not support me in experiencing a temporary disability, albeit one instigated in part by his own hands.

So, I printed my driving history (containing one or two speeding tickets) and took it with my resume, filled mainly with legal experience, to the car dealership. I thought it would be fun, and the last time I'd had a lot of fun working was as a cocktail waitress for just over a year during law school.

My dad had gone to an event at the recently opened Seattle W Hotel and told me I would like it and to go check it out for work. That time, he was right on. I loved it. I applied, and by playing up my experience of waitressing at the golf course, I got hired as a cocktail server. I worked in the bar, which was nestled between the restaurant and lobby, where we also served sometimes all the way to the chairs that sat up the lobby stairs leading to the front desk and concierge. I bought books about mixed drinks to learn all the spirits as well as I'd represented in the interview. It was fun while it lasted, and we pooled our tips—in my best two weeks and part-time, I made $3,000 in just tips. W means "whatever/whenever," and we could treat the guests as creatively as possible. I was even allowed, upon my suggestion, to buy Christmas presents for our regulars. A star for Jonathan, who lit up the bar with his smile and laughter. Desk clocks from Restoration Hardware for the two doctors from Virginia Mason who always stopped by on their way downhill to their ferry and, like clockwork, paid and went on their timely way.

In the vein of whatever/whenever, I once chased a guest, literally running after him. He accidentally left his credit card behind. The bell guys pointed me up the block. I waited at the bottom of the parking garage until he saw me at the pay booth, where I returned his credit card. He was completely shocked that I would do something like that. The following week, he brought me a beautiful orange swirly Swedish glass blown votive holder in gratitude. I also overheard guests complaining about having been scolded for asking for salt and pepper as they dined in our hotel restaurant. As I joined my coworker Jess and listened, the wife explained, *"We have simple tastes; we would be happy with macaroni and cheese!"* Via their bar tab, I discerned their room number, but I was about to get off my shift. I grabbed Ted the bell guy: *"Here's some cash, go down the street to the twenty-four-hour corner store, buy a pack of macaroni and cheese, go to room --- and deliver it, promising we will make Chef cook it for them anytime they want."* He acted like he had never heard of such a crazy and seemingly senseless idea. Fortunately, he did it anyway. The wife, who opened the door, saw the box, heard what he said, and gave him a huge hug—and a Benjamin—as gratuity.

Near the end, I was dating JD and still working there. A group of business guys from the East Coast, I think, came into our bar to party but were staying at another hotel. The married ones eventually went back to their place, but two stayed and tried picking up a couple of girls who were our hotel guests. They seemed slightly irritated to have their table invaded, so I made the rule that if they joined the ladies, they were responsible for their entire tab. The girls smiled, the guys joined them, and the girls ordered three or four trays of ice topped with twenty oysters on the half shell. It came up that I was dating a pilot, and the louder guy said, *"Ha-ha, your guy flies around, but I get flown around,"* and it was on. I was miffed. I was motivated to even the score. It came to me after the girls scurried up to their rooms, to the guys' dismay. I went to the front desk and asked for one non-coded room key and a blank key envelope. We had fifteen floors, so I wrote something like 1612 on the outside. They were drunk, but I figured upon elevator entry, they would *"get it"* because there was no sixteenth floor. I told the bartender, John about my plan and planned to hide downstairs after delivering the key so as not to give away the prank or face their wrath. I was fully prepared to get fired. The next night, the entire group returned, saw me, and cheered. Hugged me, even. They had figured the 16 was a mistake, and the girls were somewhere on the fifteenth floor. They were trying the key and knocking on doors until security escorted them out. They had never been so successfully pranked and loved me for it. A sneaky prank became a surprise success!

As I left for the car sales interview, JD asked me where I found the job listing. When I explained, he said I'd never get the job. I said, *"Watch me."* I was intrigued by the ad, which implied substantial compensation related to commission and even benefits. I also loved new cars, and I loved shopping. I was going to be a personal shopper for cars. Easy. Practicing law, I was used to the idea of not knowing how much I would make each month. Unlimited potential to earn excited me. When I went in for the interview, I totally expected to be the only girl. It turned out that I was one of three girls in a group of about a dozen people. I wasn't the only girl, and not the only blonde either. We were all hired, because I later learned that selling cars is something you can either do or you can't. All of us came from other backgrounds, and we were promised training before being allowed to go on the sales floor to work with a live customer. To some extent, the new people were also used to catch customers from leaving the lot. That way, senior salespeople could complete the parts of the process that the temporary salespeople couldn't handle.

On my first day after being released from training, I sold a truck to one of the nicest guys I've ever met, a Samoan man named George. He had a great time picturing himself in a new Dakota pickup, and if the bank approved, he would sign up. He was so pleased with the experience he later brought in a huge tray of Samoan barbeque and regularly said hello every time he visited the dealership. Other customers, Sunshine and Mark, sent me thank-you flowers. One beautiful couple, Joe and Gregory, even had me over for a lovely Christmas dinner after buying three cars from me.

I was thrilled to have found a profession where I could make a deal in one day, after as little as four hours, having come from law, where it could take over a year just to draft a settlement that resulted after two to three years of litigation and negotiation. Bam, deal, you just bought a car. Awesome. I didn't know much about cars and got good at reading the window sticker, the Monroney sticker, backwards while sitting in the back during the customer's test drive and answering questions on the fly. (Monroney, thanks to a legal battle over some guy named Monroney who probably didn't disclose all the car's attributes at the time of a sale.) I was also great at not acknowledging the word "no." This is essential in sales, as it has been in my life, to discover a way when being told otherwise.

One customer only said *"yes"* the moment that she agreed to buy the truck. Not a single yes preceded that ultimate final affirmation. One of the guys turned her over to me after three no's. He said he wasn't getting anywhere with her and had to give someone else a try. She seemed to be the sweetest grandma type, but she seemed tough and resistant at the same time. She refused a test drive, so instead, I told her and her husband to *"Get in!"* I spoke firmly but nicely at the same time as if it would be fun. And they did. Then, I told him to hand over his license, and he did. I said I'd be back with the keys, and of course, I also brought a prefilled test-drive form in two copies so I could leave one at the manager's desk as we passed by the main entrance on our way out on the test drive they'd flatly refused minutes earlier. While waiting for me to return from dropping a signed drive form, the truck ran out of gas! Mortified, I told them to see numbers while we got it handled. After shaking my and my manager's hands, she hesitated for a second, saying, *"Wait a minute, we didn't even get to drive the truck."* Her husband smirked and said, *"Yes, we did. We drove it across the lot!"*

The less I believed the words coming out of people's mouths. The more I paid attention to the way they lit up when they looked at a car or how they smiled at each other across the console during a test drive as they asked each other if they liked a car, the easier it was for me just to continue accompanying them along the sales process. Their hesitation or resistance was just fear in a process they ultimately wanted to or sometimes needed to accomplish. And I was their willing guide.

Over the year or so, I was selling cars; I was almost fired, I think, three times. Ironically, I was happy to have had those close calls. Once or twice, it was for not putting out enough effort because they knew I had greater potential. This was not like the B+ talk my dad had given me in fourth grade, where I wasn't giving my best last 10% of the effort. This was me totally being distracted by my gloomy personal life, a bit lazy, and generally unmotivated to the point of giving more like 30% total effort—so totally a reasonable conversation. Once, I also misused one of the dealer license plates, but I pled the fifth, learned my lesson, and didn't get fired that time either. What those close calls showed me, though, was that part of me was back. I'd almost been sent home three times in Australia as an exchange student, too. Again, I must plead the fifth, but I think the statute of limitations on those times is now safely passed. I can say drinking was involved each time. Still, I realized that selling cars somehow was part of what continued allowing my quintessential self to reemerge after having been smothered for the last decade and a half because of living society's expectations while serving others instead of tuning into my own, eventually desperate, needs.

Twice, I took breaks from the car sales, once by choice, and once not so much.

Chapter 12

THE DEATH THREAT

I had only been selling cars for about two months. JD was home from work, and I was coming home late from an off-site car sale. For these sales, we would move all the used cars to a lot on a main road in a nearby town. People would be lured in with mailers that were more like baited hooks for fish with little chance of finding their own food or car purchases due to credit challenges. Still, some of the demographic would bring friends, family, or significant others to cosign, and some could qualify for first-time buyer programs, etc. Off-site sales meant later nights for me because, away from the dealership, the managers would hang around and talk at the end of the night. I was in no rush to go home to a distant, cold, and grumpier-by-the-day husband.

I pushed it. I was sleeping as little as four or five hours, even smelling like cigarette smoke, hoping JD would take notice, especially given my history of sleep deprivation issues. He didn't. It seemed like I wasn't even on his radar. I couldn't let him go back to work without sorting things out once and for all. It was like I needed him to read the writing on the wall for me. I pushed him, and like an angry bear, he roared back. He had been hibernating in our room, glued to his computer while sitting on the bed, in his little den of disgust with his life's circumstances as he approached forty. I drank a few beers after getting home from work, stood in the doorway of our small master bedroom, and asked him point blank what he wanted.

I was working like he'd demanded, but that didn't seem to have made any difference in his behavior toward me. He said he wanted a divorce. There, he finally said it. He wanted a divorce. The D-word. The scarlet D. He said he was upset about our finances and that he thought his poor credit rating was the reason that his resume was passed up for the possibility of an interview at FedEx (his ideal dream). Somehow, I found the words to continue, quickly pondering what would be the only ways I would consider leaving the door to reconciliation open. *"Would you ever consider not flying?"* I asked.

"No, it's what I'm good at. I'm the best, and I've got skills in the cockpit. There's nothing else I'll do for a career."

Second question. *"What's the most important thing to you?"*

"Money."

He listed others I can't recall, but the top slot was money. Not God, not family. Both were wrong answers, where I could finally draw lines in places I'd previously not perceived to be necessary for my self-preservation and fulfillment. But he didn't stop there; he glared at me with the glow of his computer, highlighting the contours of his face from below. He was so desperate and so in need of bringing me there with him that he said the worst words I'd ever hear come from his or anyone's mouth.

"I'm so upset at you, Sarah; you have no idea. I'm so upset right now that I could kill you and myself," he snarled with force enough to accomplish the job.

I was stunned at how serious he sounded and quickly remembered that he was the only one who knew where his gun was in the house. Stunned at how his threat was more like a plan. Not just to kill me, but to kill himself too. Classic premeditation.

How many times had I read headlines where that occurred, someone taking others out before themselves? There was nothing left to say.

It was time for me to leave, but I had to sober up, sleep (hah), pack, and find a place to go. Now I notice how it didn't even occur to me to call 9-1-1 and have him instantly removed from the home. I didn't know domestic violence when it was yelling at me in the face. How could I not see it, even as a lawyer? The ability to be objective or logical escaped me. I got JD to agree to sleep upstairs again and locked myself in our room with Teddy. I figured if he shot his gun through the wall, he'd probably miss. That's exactly what went through my sleep-deprived mind.

I called for backup, but I soon discovered I called for the wrong kind. The people I'd been hiding everything from, for good reason, only confirmed those reasons within a few sentences of my call.

I dialed a number I'd rarely dialed in the last year but of course, still knew by heart. Even before my brother's wedding, I'd stopped attending the family events. I'd skipped my grandma's birthday that last July because I was sick of the implied guilt and shame for not attending an event. *"We missed you at 'x,'"* they would say, and yet I would hear *how dare you are not there and disappoint us*. I once counted dozens of holidays, birthdays, and other family celebrations each year. We were not "required" to get together more than twice a month for such events. Events that were draining me physically, mentally, and emotionally. While I made my appearances and maintained the expected cheery, complacent façade, I also missed work and put in extra hours to make up and keep the house as close to JD's standards as possible at the same time. I was so committed to my clients, family, and even the community through Rotary and as a small business owner employing others that there was no time or room for self-care, let alone self-reflection, in my life. It wasn't long after meeting my therapist, Kari, that she handed me *The Giving Tree*. Upon finishing a reread, she asked me, *"Now, did the boy love the tree?"*

"Yes," was my immediate answer. The tabletop fountain in her yellow-walled and small, intimate office bubbled in the silence. I had somehow been the tree, but upon my demise, I felt I had even been de-stumped and used for wood chips. All that was left were the roots. I was the roots. Roots in mud. (Now I know what grows from roots, but I didn't for a long time.)

So, roots made a call. It was 3:30 a.m., but they eventually answered. Mom then Dad got on the phone, groggy, but together. I verbally purged, *"The reason I couldn't sleep and took all the pills last year is because JD cheated on me. We are getting a divorce, and he just threatened to kill me. I need to leave."*

Mom spoke in a monotone. *"We're not coming; we're not going to help you. You're going to have to figure this out on your own,"* or the equivalent, she said in a steady, careful voice, with an almost practiced-sounding word choice, as if she'd studied a worksheet they hand out at the support group for people with a bipolar child.

Dad took things to the next level. *"Well, now I'm worried about the salvation of your soul because you're going to hell."* These were his exact words, which I wish I never heard.

There. There were the parents I had been avoiding facing. There was the absence of unconditional support and non-judgment I'd anticipated. It hurt, but at the same time, it affirmed the cause of my anxiety. My gut instinct was strangely vindicated, but I was still desperate.

But I needed a place to go. A place where I felt safe, so I could just sleep, take two weeks off work and be able to sleep. I wouldn't take no for an answer. Maybe it was the late/early hour, but they relented. I could meet my sister downtown to get condo keys and stay there later that day after I slept and packed up. Now I wonder whether they believed me about the threat because they, too, a judge and his wife, didn't recommend I call the police after a serious threat to my life in an obvious domestic violence scenario. Had my dad and I really passed the bar? This issue was so obvious any law student could spot it. Regardless, I made sure to get out of the house before JD made it downstairs. Teddy and I were homeless, and with whatever I quickly packed for us, we fled to the condo in my pearl white Infiniti FX35, a color I had chosen because it reminded me of my ivory silk wedding dress.

Chapter 13

THE CHALLENGE OF SLEEP DEPRIVATION

Since my sister had moved out with her new husband and a renter had yet to move in, Mom and Dad's fifth-floor Belltown condo was conveniently vacant. I took in its southerly view of downtown Seattle, with a slanted view of the water. West Seattle shimmered back at me in the distance. My sister had it good here, a purchase made possible after JD and I bought the Sumner two-story starter home from Mom and Dad. They chose to 1031 exchange their profit—of course, they profited—and as a result, they bought this one-bedroom downtown perch. Initially, I felt safe. That was the main thing. Sleep was secondary. But I'd visited my sister before, and her old double bed was still there. It was comfortable, and the vintage wrought iron frame was back to white, her choice of paint color after yellow, pink, purple—almost the whole rainbow had at one point colored that iron. Instead, the walls were purple. Purple and teal were colors she'd always favored, and both brought out different flecks in her hazel eyes. It was like she still felt nearby, and that was comforting. Still, sleep was a challenge.

The first night, I tried alcohol. I went downstairs to the street-level Italian restaurant, which had just locked its doors. Sebastian, a friend of my sister's, who also happened to be nearer our father's age than mine, was inside. I banged on the glass door. *"Please let me in. I'm hungry, and I'm getting a divorce!"*

He opened the door laughing and obliged with food and plenty of alcohol. He invited me to a nearby bar for more drinks, where I fell into a blurry conversation with a purple-hearted soldier, who I accidentally kissed out in front of the bar when we went out for a smoke. Sebastian came to the pseudo-rescue. He stepped in and walked me home but went in for his opening after offering another drink in the closed restaurant before I bolted upstairs and passed out. Not having slept nearly enough, I arranged for a couple of weeks off work and contemplated what else might quickly assist in my quest for some z's. I went to the pharmacy and bought some Tylenol PM. I figured it couldn't hurt might be more like Benadryl, which wasn't really working for me. However, when I got back to the condo to try the next night, I suddenly burst into tears.

I was scared shitless that the Tylenol PM could result in side effects or even rebound insomnia like the Ambien had. I called Amy, my friend since we became neighbors in third grade. She was a pharmacist. We were so high achieving in our neighborhood; one neighbor had become a food scientist, another a lawyer and a veterinarian, not to mention my siblings and the six or more degrees, including law between them. The snobs from the hill, at least that's how I think they saw us girls. Amy reassured me through my small waterfall of fear that it was safe to try the Tylenol PM and that I would be fine. Neither of us then recognized what I might need more, just to get away, take a break, a real and long break to settle down without stewing in the stress pond my life had again become. Not only was I still grieving the losses of the past year, but I was still struggling to recover from the torture of the tricked hospitalization and holding facility while facing divorce and my grandma's imminent death. Whatever I really needed, Tylenol PM was not it. And it didn't work. Not much at all.

Unfortunately, I still felt the need to get back to work, then more than ever because I was losing JD, his extra financial support, and possibly the house as well. I didn't know if I would get or could live in the house, the place where so much emotional pain had been initiated and had yet to be healed. So, to be able to return to work promptly, sleep was a requirement, and the more I needed it, the more it escaped me. I went to my psychiatrist for yet another prescription and to confirm whether I was manic. He heard me out and listened to how I had been feeling and what was happening. In the two days since I'd made it to Seattle, things felt stranger again. I was very anxious and easily distracted, and normal things like buildings and signs began to feel otherworldly. He had diagnosed me with adjustment disorder, basically breaking down in the face of severe trauma. It's a temporary diagnosis, and recovery naturally occurs within three to six months of the trauma subsiding. My trauma with JD was reignited by the death threat and decision to divorce, and it was intensified by the somewhat intentional loss of my law office. My grandma's rapidly approaching demise, especially when the conflict with my parents prevented JD from accompanying me to visit her. I hadn't seen her since before her last birthday, probably since the previous June. My best friend Jennah drove me to the doctor's appointment. Her mother was in town and rode with us. I was so easily distracted and anxious I didn't feel safe driving that far of a distance. This time, upon my insistence that I get better fast enough to return to work sooner rather than later, I was prescribed lithium. My blood would need to be tested, and then I could start the meds that were supposed to keep me level and low enough, hopefully, to sleep. Since we naturally absorb lithium from the rays of a setting sun, I was most comfortable trying that as opposed to other suggestions.

At the hospital in Bellevue where I went to get tested, I got lost two or three times, walking around to find the blood draw office. That wasn't the only reason I took forever to get back to Jennah and her mom, who were waiting outside in her gray Saab. I met Gigi Reed in one of the lobbies. She was a jewelry designer doing a special sale that, in part, raised money for something related to children and the hospital. I tapped into part of my office business account, instead of losing or being credited with half the funds in the divorce, to purchase about $1,000 in jewelry that I liked. JD never bought me jewelry that I liked other than my engagement setting and wedding band, which I approved of at the time of purchase. He would come home from work with little gift sets of inexpensive costume jewelry, maybe now as a small way of apologizing for a transgression. Maybe he never knew how much I disliked them, but I didn't wear any of them and, as my grandma always said, look what they do, not what they say.

Back at the condo with another bottle of pills that were supposed to help me, I froze up again. The little pink capsules were supposed to be taken at the same time every day to keep your body's dosage level. Somewhere inside, I knew this wasn't what I needed. This wasn't going to work. But I was more desperate and needed myself back faster than I thought I could get *"back"* on my own (three to six months being the typical natural recovery period for adjustment disorder). I called the pharmacist. Not my friend. I didn't want her to know what I was taking, so I called the one who filled my prescription at the Walgreens down the street. She said lithium works, but only if you trust it and let it work. That would not be easy for me, but I could try. I took them, but only for two or three days, again not feeling myself and not feeling it was right. I poured all of them into the toilet and watched them expand like the little sponge animals we used to soak in water as kids, always surprised at the zoo that was hidden within the multicolored clear-coated pills.

I took a picture of the pink polka-dotted toilet water, texted it to my parents, and flushed. My parents told me they were coming to the condo and, if I didn't allow them in, they would remove me by police force.

Chapter 14

MEETING BEN

I was now staying at the Vintage Park, where I used to take advantage of the cheap valet working downtown at the attorney general's office during law school. The same cute guys took my Infiniti as I moved into my new temporary home. It was an intimate setting and reminded me a little of when I lived in a pensione in Florence, Italy, during college, but in a nicer room with a bathroom of my own. They even allowed dogs, as Teddy was still by my side. My parents, to me valuing their property over their daughter, threatened to remove me from their condo by police force if I didn't go willingly. All I asked was to stay there alone for two uninterrupted weeks to sleep. To sleep. And to get a break, and get back into my house, then go back to work as things settled down. Instead, they had to come. They needed to access the condo, probably to make sure I wasn't destroying it in the *"bipolar"* crazed mental state they thought I was in. Granted, I had drawn with a Sharpie all over the bar countertop at the house. JD and I shared and wrote on some mirrors when I came home from the hospital the first time, but no one noticed that the places where I wrote were also easily cleaned, as if it hadn't happened at all. If only it were that easy to erase other things... I was in nowhere near the condition I had been after coming home from the hospital, suffering the side effects of a half dozen medications, but my parents didn't know that. They still subscribed to the bipolar diagnosis and seemed to be attending some bipolar family member support groups. They were treating me at arm's length as if I was something to be dealt with clinically. Instead, I was freshly traumatized and still suffering from my more accurately diagnosed adjustment disorder. I just needed space to decompress, de-stress, feel safe, and sleep. Sleep.

My former law partner's brother, Brad, helped me move from the condo to Vintage Park and offered unconditional support and assistance. He would help me find an apartment if I couldn't move home. He didn't judge and, like a guardian angel, made sure I safely moved to my new temporary home. He even drove my car there for me because I felt too anxious and distracted to drive. First, JD threatened to kill me; then, my parents threatened the police force. Unreal.

I talked a little bit to my aunt, my dad's older and only sister. She was recently divorced, too—and so Catholic she is even a Carmelite nun, the kind of nun that could be married. She had moved back to southern California from Minnesota to be away from her ex-husband. Aunt Grace understood my fears. She was on Team Sarah and especially understood how it felt to have been judged and treated like a lower-value human by my dad. Dad always valued her as being correct on all things Catholic but totally off base and crazy about pretty much everything else. Because she was a human who expressed feelings not just in words but with authenticity from her being, from true joy to pure sadness, he was unable to relate. He treated her like she lived in a parallel universe. For years, it was acceptable to disregard her unless it was a church issue. They kept infrequent contact, and I later learned all her attempts to reach out in writing desperately fell on deaf ears. At any rate, she was sure to inform me that I wasn't allowed to date or even so much as kiss someone until my annulment was processed by the church, and that could take years. Years. My civil divorce wasn't even filed. The writing of inevitable divorce was on the wall, yet it would be years, according to the church, before I could morally and without sin date again. I was mortified. I remembered confessing having had premarital sex with JD and the priest making me cry. This was not going to be easy, but I'd do my best. My best, according to my dad, was damn near perfection, but in this case, I suspected I'd settle for less. I had to live free. I was scared but newly free of my marriage and having to run a law office. Would it require freedom from the church, too, to move on in the ways I was yearning for?

I was walking Teddy, and we were making a loop around the Fairmont when a cute, young, sandy blond-haired guy asked me for a light or a cigarette, I don't remember which. Later I found out he noticed me because of my khaki green cargo pants. He loves pockets so much that in another life, he could have been a kangaroo. Ben James looked like a combination of all the guys I'd had a crush on in high school, and he wasn't much older, just twenty-three compared to my decade or so more years. We started talking. At first, I thought I'd help him find work, maybe selling cars if he wanted to, because they would give anyone a chance at it. I immediately could feel how kind his heart was and how caring he was as a person. I sensed it was innate to his nature, even before I learned that he'd moved to the West Coast to help his grandmother recover from an illness. He was supposed to be starting work at a new job but instead readily agreed to drive me to my doctor's appointments. He needed work, and I needed a driver. After hanging out for a day, one appointment attended; he let me get him a room at a nearby hotel for one night before he ended up just staying with me.

In the back of my mind, I'd always thought if something happened to JD, then I would go for someone younger. But by something happening, I figured JD might die—maybe flying in and out of Afghanistan delivering cargo or in some bizarre flight incident. I never saw it coming that we'd separate over his cheating and an eventual impasse of values and moral differences. As JD got older, he got grumpier, more tired, and took less care of himself on the road. Younger was the way I always secretly planned to go, and younger Ben was!

But according to my aunt, I was in a pickle. It was the weekend of Easter, and Jennah's baptism was to be on Easter vigil. I was her sponsor. I realize now her entry was the beginning of my exit. It was like a spiritual substitution. Take her, let me go. Like my brother's wedding less than a year earlier, I felt I had to attend and stand up as her sponsor. Never mind that I was in the middle of my round two breakdown while on the run from my parents and a threatening ex. I couldn't find it in me to say, *"No, I can't be there; I have my own shit to handle."* I tried asking my parents not to go because their presence would freak me out, but of course, they wouldn't agree to that. They were there. So was Ben. He went with me and even took out his lower lip piercing to put on a better show for the judge and his wife. He wore the clothes I got him for the occasion, bought with the cash I got from pawning my wedding rings.

I had wanted to throw them into Puget Sound off one of the piers along the waterfront. He convinced me not to. I let him take me to Johnson's Jewelry, where I'd gotten the wedding band and asked John, my former law partner's trusted and good friend, what pawn shop he recommended. Months later, when I tried to retrieve the rings just after the deadline, I found out that the stone in my engagement setting had been a fake. A good fake called moissanite was only detected by removing and weighing the stone, but a fake indeed. Neither of us knew at the time because we bought the rock together. Still, my ring was as fake as his commitment to the vows of marriage turned out to be.

I participated in the mass as if I was on autopilot. I was there for Jennah, standing up for her as I was melting down. I was practically hallucinating again as if I could see all the angels and saints hovering above us during the vigil while listening to the music, the priest's words, her dunking, and the recital of the baptismal affirmations of the faith.

Ben and I briefly and accidentally crossed paths with my parents after the vigil, but I could have jumped out of my skin. I was so anxious and uncomfortable to have them so near me. We quickly walked away at my quiet but obvious urging, which Ben naturally and easily picked up on. From our first drive together, he picked up on my every breath. He'd ask what was wrong or if I was okay if I just breathed differently or ever-so-slightly sighed just one time. He caught me so early in my feelings that it was easy to share with him at that moment before I ruminated on it and stored it away. It was the opposite of my experience to that point. Away from my parents, I felt jostled and scared. I was scared of what was next because, of course, I wanted what was next to be that we had sex that night. But also recalling my aunt's admonition, I asked him to marry me on the side of the church. He readily agreed—the ride I was on, he was in—and we went back to the church and asked the priest who'd just baptized Jennah for help. He had us wait a few minutes in the back of the church; then he took us up to the left front side of the church. A huge mosaic, a blonde depiction of Mary, hovered on the wall behind him as he took us through what felt like a Romeo-and-Juliet-like secret wedding ceremony. Of course, there was no way to really marry us, but we'd told him a story like we'd known each other for so long and finally wanted to be together. He was lit up by the excitement of the Easter vigil service and was taken in. After he finished with us, Ben and I kissed for the first time, then walked back to the W where I had gotten him a room for more.

It was fun and weird having sex with someone besides JD for the first time; almost like starting over because it was so different. Ben had a '*culo di marmo*' (an ass that "belongs on a statue," in Italian slang) and the chiseled, muscular body of the David to go with it. Not to mention, he was more than twice as large and as hard as I was used to. It was freeing to be with him, though, like our sexual union affirmed the marital separation that JD said he wanted. I willingly agreed to the divorce, as I'd agreed to so many requests from others over the years. Later, I wished I'd participated more intentionally in the decision to end things, but now it almost feels as if I had anyway.

Divorce had just not been in my vocabulary, as if never uttering the word meant it was not an option in my world. I had believed in the vows and that because we'd taken them before God, an unbreakable bond had been formed. But for the bond to be truly unbreakable, we both had to believe that to be so. JD had said so in words but not in actions. And some of my grandma's best advice was, *"Look what they do, not what they say."* What he had done could not be undone, and neither could the avalanche of events that he'd catalyzed.

Ben had the street smarts equivalent of my book smarts, and he appealed to my adventurous and sneaky side. Meeting new people was always fun for me, but he was a new kind of person, the kind I wasn't open to before because of my upbringing. But he was the kind of person I needed exactly at that moment and later would need even more.

I know now that one of my dad's worst fears, besides losing me to suicide, used to be that I would have a baby with Ben. Still, he would suck it up and do things like email me to say, *"It was good seeing you and Ben,"* as if Ben and I were still an item of some sort. It made me feel safer not letting my parents in on the details of my life, so whatever he gathered about my circumstances would remain tidbits he came across. It's almost like a game of telephone, where what he thought he knew was sometimes radically distanced from the truth. I have not found his past reactions to the truth to be supportive, as if he never had an example of how to be that way. All I've heard about his upbringing sounds like something out of *Leave It to Beaver*, a classic 1950s black-and-white television experience, which he looks back on as if it were the ideal standard against which all childhood could be measured.

Like Olympic medals, my dad displayed the three of us kids to the world. Our podiums were on the wall of his office and, last I saw, still on the wall of his judicial chambers. Framed cork boards with our names inscribed on gold plates at the base of each frame: Sarah | Jason | Lily. Most people survive the death of their parents. I felt like I had to survive my dad before he died.

I had not been authentically myself since returning home from Australia. It was as if I lived to fit the shape of my containers instead of living from my heart. I'd met Erin Brockovich years earlier at some lawyers' dinner in Seattle. When I saw that she was coming to talk to WSTLA, I insisted to my then-partner Jackie that we attend. Just to be in the room with her would be inspirational osmosis, I thought. Not only did we attend, but we got to say hello to Erin after hearing her speak. She was warm and lovely and signed my program for me: *"Dear Sarah, Follow your heart! Love, Erin."* What perfectly simple advice.

Everything was made more difficult by being viewed through a bipolar filter and because of my parents' apparent faith in my inevitable suicide. They also seemed to believe that if it weren't for the trauma of JD cheating and the medications after that, I would have gone on to live a perfectly normal life instead of having to come to grips with living bipolar. *"It's okay to have bipolar, Sarah,"* my dad encouraged, *"even Catherine Zeta-Jones came out as having bipolar."* Awesome, Dad, but what if I'm not? What if Mr. thirty-year practicing doctor at St. Joseph's was wrong? Or is that as beyond the scope of your world as a failure, such as divorce, had been in mine?

Since I was most myself when I lived over ten thousand miles away, my parents were unfamiliar with me living as me. They were pleased with façade-me. And to keep them comfortable, keep the peace, avoid their judgment, criticism and shame, I would oblige and put on the façade they were comfortable with whenever in His Honor's presence: The girl who didn't sleep with her husband before marriage. Who didn't almost get sent home three times from Australia? Who wasn't almost raped in Australia with only herself to protect her? Who never cheated in school. Who didn't prefer yoga to golf and horseback riding or prefer meditation over mass? Who didn't color her hair bright red, blue, pink, or purple? Who didn't pierce anything other than earlobes? Who would never get a divorce, never have a tattoo, never partake in marijuana, or occasionally enjoy casual sex? Who never had any sort of threesome or any fun on a plane? Who would not get a drink and then make out with her hiring manager on the day of her interview? Who wasn't almost fired three times from a car sales job? Who never vandalized property or smoked cigarettes. Who never defaulted on her debts. But who was an honorable officer of the court, a member of the Rotary and golf clubs, a Catholic and dutiful wife, eventual mother, and spitting image of them?

Chapter 15

FIRST ATTEMPT

In the middle of the night, while Ben was asleep, I snuck out of the Vintage Park Hotel bed and went into the bathroom. I tried lying on the floor and meditating myself to sleep. The cold floor pressed up against me through the plush white towel. It wasn't working, so I turned some music on low from my phone and ran the hot water to fill the tub and steam up the room like the hot yoga studio. Maybe the heat would help, and a quick soak. Bored, waiting for the tub to fill, I drew on the steamy bathroom mirror, what looked like angel wings complete with feathers because of the remnants of tissue half stuck to the wet surface. Intrigued by my accidental creation, I took a few pictures with my phone, then got back to attempting some yoga on the floor. Whatever felt good: cat/cow, breathing, stretching, trying to physically release the anxiety and fear of knowing that my parents were back in town to secure their precious condo and try God knows what with me. I had the other hotel fax a copy of Ben's driver's license to my dad's office so that he could go ahead and background-check the guy I was hanging out with. I almost fell asleep in the hot tub, then decided to take pictures of the soap-bubbly water before crawling back into bed. Everything felt surreal and real, and deep sleep remained just out of reach.

Before Ben woke up, I snuck out of the room, leaving some room-service breakfast bedside for him. I had to get home, and the only way my anxious, exhausted mind could figure out that might happen was with a restraining order. I had one of the bellmen escort me to a lawyer's office downtown. Even walking across the street felt unsafe because I was such a wreck. Ben needed to sleep, and I wanted help going in a different direction if I accidentally crossed paths with my parents.

I wore my leather trench and a scarf; my makeup was intact until I started spilling my guts to the lawyer in the conference room. It was a typical downtown office on an upper floor, conservatively decorated enough to maintain a businesslike, highly professional environment while attempting to soothe clients at the same time. There was a part of my story where I explained that I learned about their office because of my dad. Upon discovering my father's connection and because I was such a blubbering mess—and I like to think because the lawyer was trying to help me—instead of preparing a restraining order, he called my dad.

"No, she doesn't need legal assistance; she needs to be committed," my dad must have conveyed. *"She has bipolar disorder and on a rage of some kind,"* he must have said. They must have ordered. What attorney doesn't follow a judge's order, and, in this case, for the care of his daughter? Ben had arrived at the law office because I left him a note about where I was. He had to wait in the lobby while I was interviewed by paramedics, who then cuffed me to a bed and removed me from the building by a stretcher on wheels to a waiting ambulance to a hospital. Since the last attempt, when I'd just tried to get an ultrasound, I could rely on the coaching I'd gotten from my attorney about how to pass the interview of the MHP (Mental Health Professional). But it was also that I was

simply not a danger to myself or others that I got released at that time. I was only diagnosed with a bladder infection, either from sex with Ben or the bubble bath or both. I was concerned my test would also show positive for marijuana because he'd already been teaching me how to smoke, but it didn't prevent my release. We went back to the Vintage Park, where my parents knew I was staying, and arranged to leave for somewhere they wouldn't know, probably the Westin.

Thankfully, I had funds from my car sales and my office that could sustain me until I returned to work. I also used Nordstrom as a *"bank"* by buying expensive items that I could easily return later, knowing this would help me to appear broke as the divorce proceeding was initiated. I could more reasonably argue for financial support. These were the things I came up with while supposedly totally in a manic rage, as seen by my parents. These were the types of things that they judged as bizarre and led to my version of hell on Earth.

Chapter 16

SCRAMBLING FOR HELP

During the general time frame of sometime after that attempt to commit me from the lawyer's office and before I was ultimately physically herded into a corner of the downtown Nordstrom, I took Ben on what probably felt like back-to-back wild goose chases. Thankfully, he stayed with me from beginning to end. I was an animated train wreck, or Humpty Dumpty, running around in pieces, trying to find a safe place and way to put myself back together. I reached out to several friends at many different times. I'm not sure I could ever fully piece together exactly when these instances really went down.

Justine and Andrea.

Post-meeting Ben and pre-involuntary incarceration, I had Ben take us to Justine's house. Justine is a friend I made at Rotary in Tacoma. She is like a comet blazing through the sky of life. Justine is tall, blonde, fun, and fully alive, the twin sister I never had. She welcomed us inside, and I tried to sleep upstairs in her bed while she talked with Ben downstairs.

Then, when I couldn't sleep, Justine and I talked on her back porch while Ben washed the Infiniti in the driveway as if washing the car was a small holiday away from the reality of my continuing to melt down.

At some point, it was decided that our friend and healer Andrea should come over to help test and balance my chakras as if that might reset me to normal as easily as in a sci-fi movie. Andrea came in and gave me a loving hug as her green eyes sparkled and began assessing the situation. She had me lie down on the bed. She gently took out and held her crystal as we talked about what had already occurred. The sunlight backlit her as she stood beside me on the bed, making her appear more angelic than human to me and reigniting my fantasy of immortality. As Andrea's crystal spun above each of my chakras, I wondered aloud if I was pregnant with Ben's baby. By then recognizing my disintegrating state, she instantly said that would NOT be good. At that time, it could also have been JD's, and I secretly decided, if that were the case, to run far, far away with Ben to raise the child where JD would never discover its existence. Had he known, he would be a part of my life forever, and I feared he could hurt the child as his dad had hurt him by banishing his mom after she'd served her purpose, and as he had me. It was as if a potential pregnancy was my go-to to elevate the drama, as well as to motivate me into action when I didn't feel I had the energy to fight for myself. Fighting for my unreal unborn took me to the next level.

They left me upstairs to try and sleep. I looked around the room, unable to even close my eyes. I was fascinated with all the knickknacks that represented Justine in her room. To *"help"* her, I reorganized almost her entire room and even every piece of makeup in her bathroom while packing myself a small pile of her things that I thought would help disguise my identity as we ran away to safety. I figured her things fit me because she and I were secretly separated at birth and really were secret twins. It was insanely ridiculous and so tragically awful. My mind was behaving like the scene of a fresh and fatal car accident that you couldn't help but look at but wanted to run from at the same time. They played along with my whacked-out fantasy, and Ben proposed to me so that we could run off, with him being the presumed father of what might be a half-black child. We left Justine's formerly peaceful home in bizarre disarray, me unfortunately worse than when we'd arrived.

Justine and I talked about that day later, in February 2013, when I called her from my Grand Hyatt, Carlsbad patio. She was amazed and proud of me for being in the middle of my weekend-long *"Healing the Heart"* seminar, put on at the Chopra Center by Deepak Chopra's people. I thanked her for her help, and she hardly let me apologize for my nutty behavior. She shared her admiration for Ben, who was nearby hanging out in the room with Teddy. We reconnected with loving friendship, and I realized that she would be someone who could continue to blaze lovingly through my life sky as I could across hers, now and again, through the rest of our lives.

Tiffany

One of the other lawyers I know is Tiffany. She attended law school at Seattle U, too, but after me. I thought it was cool that we both turned out to be lawyers, as we first met as Novice Women rowers our freshman year at Gonzaga. She, too, was a young-looking Legally Blonde championing her clients while earning respect in the courtroom. I often felt underestimated and that it was something I could use to my advantage, even though it was irritating at the same time. Having shared the experience of pulling for our lives in an eight-woman boat, we knew full well each other's tenacity. I also trusted her with my desperation and story at some point, meeting her and her husband in the lobby of the W.

I felt safe at the W because of the countless hours I had spent there as a server. I knew every square inch of the lobby's wood floor, and I knew its insides. I once asked security to remove a guy who was wandering around the lobby barefoot, with tattered, dirty jeans and a worn T-shirt, because I thought he must have been a homeless street person who would rather wait inside than just outside our front entrance at the bus stop. Security again stopped me, breaking the news that he was a young Amazon.com millionaire. Alright, but can he at least wear shoes?

Sitting in the lobby by the fireplace together with Ben, Tiffany, and her husband, also an attorney, I pushed her out of her comfort zone and beyond her knowledge about my potential options. I wanted her to be able to help me as a lawyer and a friend, and she did her best to do both but lost me. In my downward spiral of doom, I slipped away at some point, letting her return to her normal life and leaving me to the black hole that I was being uncontrollably sucked into with g-forces beyond my ability to combat, regardless of those I was desperately reaching out to for help.

Saul

At one point, I decided I would file for divorce, or rather a declaration of invalidity of marriage, which is like the civil court version of a church annulment. I ran into an old friend from Rotary in Auburn, an always friendly, smart, moustache-faced, and loud-tie-wearing Saul. I had stopped by the Regional Justice Center in Kent and debated having JD meet me there to file the forms I had printed off in the law library downstairs. Instead, and before he may have realized what a total mess I was, I talked Saul into letting me meet with him at his home office. Ben drove as we followed him home. My meeting with Saul was as dreamlike and unreal as my time in the bird section at Walmart with Tyler. He agreed to keep everything confidential as I poured my temporarily disabled mind and heart out to him. I wondered if I had a claim against Rotary for being assaulted and raped while in their care years earlier as an exchange student in Australia. I revised the divorce petition forms as he sat by and reviewed my scribbled, but somewhat sensical work. I reworked them into a petition for having the court declare my marriage invalid, which I felt to be more authentic to what had happened. I also thought it was a surefire way to guarantee my church annulment. He listened, comforted, and was more a friend to me than a lawyer. He let me leave with Ben instead of in an ambulance like Belle's father on my way to an asylum, and his gentle support was part of what carried me through what was to come.

Tina

I met Tina when we were four or five years old in preschool before Sr. Claire rocked my kindergarten world. Tina and I were instantly bonded, the friend version of soulmates. We were best friends throughout elementary school, until we were separated by her parents putting her into public school sometime before fifth grade. She shared what she learned and did at public school with me, though, blowing my mind when I heard what a *"rubber"* was and about her first kisses. We continue to float in and out of each other's lives, sometimes closer than others, and will always share our sisterly bond. We spent countless hours on the phone together, watching marathons of *Brady Bunch* episodes and chatting the night away after promising to sleep when spending the night at each other's houses. We traded stickers as seriously as stockbrokers.

In college, we were roommates during our freshman year. One night, I kicked her seven-foot basketball player future husband out of our first-floor window because I was desperate to sleep as much as possible after hours of study in the library and before the crew, when I'd be on the water at 5 a.m. the next day.

Tina had me over to catch up around her birthday, in September, just when I'd begun taking all the Celexa, lorazepam, and Valium, and probably just after Jennah had left that Labor Day weekend. She noticed my strangeness, and the longer we chatted, the less she could deny I was myself. I don't remember if I slept over that night or just left late. She even drove me home at 4 or 5 a.m. after I woke and felt totally out of place in her girl's bedroom. I needed normal, and I thought going home to a normal place would help. It didn't, but she obliged and dropped me home before returning to care for her beautiful family and husband, who hadn't let my kicking him out deter him from pursuing her.

Lauren

I thought I met Lauren in sixth grade when we became almost instant friends. We were later admonished by one teacher who banned *"facial expressions"* in his classroom, at his wits' end, with our self-entertaining antics in response to his boring-to-death teachings. One day, her mom discovered that she and I had our first communion together years before, in second grade, at Holy Apostles Catholic Church. I had been the annoying girl next to her, asking what was next every five minutes because I had missed all the preparation and rehearsals while on a summer trip with my family.

A special metabolism guaranteed Lauren's tall, model-like figure. She helped at some point, taking me to banks after I discovered JD had emptied and closed accounts that he, at the time, had access to, even transferring some utility bills to my accounts without my permission. I needed to close and open new accounts that he didn't know of, and at Lauren's and my therapist Kari's direction, I got some prepaid debit cards to pace my spending so that I wouldn't run out of cash during my time off work and then initiating divorce proceedings. Lauren kept me from repeating the sleep-shopping sprees I had been on the previous fall and mother-birded me to the next phase of my tragic adventure. Unfortunately, neither she nor anyone else—especially not me—could prevent the darkness from coming.

I later learned through Lauren how pissed off JD was when I shared that I was afraid I had been raped after the nightmares

I had while staying at Recovery Innovations. He was angry that I might not really have been a virgin when we met. Like he got bad goods. I was a fake, just like my diamond turned out to be. Lauren, of course, thought that was awful. My nightmare, making him angry.

Mindy

Mindy was an instant best friend from the time my family moved when I was in third grade to the cul-de-sac neighborhood where Amy and Scott, also my age, were neighbors and instant friends. While Ben was driving me from Oregon to Washington and back two, maybe even three, times before my parents eventually netted me, there were some calls made to Mindy. She lives across the state in the Tri-Cities with her four kids and husband, preventing her from coming over in person to help. I'm sad, sorry, and embarrassed for the calls that Mindy took from both Ben and me, while at times I was crazily driving at beyond highway speeds before abruptly stopping, hoping maybe that a fast stop would also stop the insanity of my life. Mindy's worry, prayers, and support from a distance were also part of what kept me afloat.

Jennifer

Jennifer lived far away, in Florida, but I called on her to join Team Sarah sometime after getting home from the Recovery Innovations experience. I had been at her wedding earlier that year. We were instant friends and then quick roommates after meeting at the W while I cocktail-served with her in law school. She listened, consoled, and referred me to her prior doctor in Seattle, who was a naturopath. I made an appointment, and Jennifer even fronted me the cash for the initial evaluation and appointment. I learned that I was light and that I had to come to terms with and make peace with my dark side. Also, I had to let JD go without a fight when the time came. It was the opposite of my meeting with Father Dan, and I was not convinced. I did take her recommendation to increase my daily fish oil intake to help maintain my mental health.

Ed

There was a time I would have expected Ed to be on this list of at least a dozen names. But who's not there now speaks volumes. He would have been there, had I reached out, of that I'm certain. I came close by getting the assistance of his brother, Henry, whose name I'd seen so many times above my own on the letterhead or below mine on pleadings. To me, he was the perfect and entertaining combination of the attorney in *Erin Brockovich* and Dicky Fox, the mentor in *Jerry Maguire*. His gruffness and abrasiveness had lessened over time, but he could still get red-faced and worked up, yelling and slamming phones on occasion. At the same time, one visit from his bright blonde toddler granddaughter instantly turned him into mush. With over twenty-five years in practice when I met him, he was from the time of the greats, closer to my dad's era, when the law was, to me, more about what was right than about making money. I had feared working in a downtown firm, banished to the basement to do all the senior partners' research without seeing the light of day, let alone the fluorescent interior rays of a courtroom. I was overjoyed to learn from and so closely be mentored by someone who didn't test actions on the mere level of the ethical rules but on what he called the *"TV Test."* If this played out on TV, how would it seem to the audience? He was always into the office early enough to shave, sometimes clip his nails, and put on his tie, ready to greet and advise clients, strategize, and send Jackie and I, his soldiers, off to war.

Ed-isms were abundant. Our meticulous assistants might have kept a list. The one that still bubbles up over and over in my mind is, "It's six of one, half dozen of another." He always called me *"SS"* in the *"red flash,"* my first little red BMW that I loved. SS, not for my initials, Sarah Small, but for Silver Spoon, which he dubbed me from the start. He also always told me: *"You have the world by the tail with a downhill pull."* How I always longed to believe him, because I had yet to feel it.

I remember riding in the car with Ed on our way to an in-home appointment for elderly clients who requested an estate plan. As he easily navigated his older, but still subtly posh, shimmering gold Chrysler 300 around the streets of Auburn, a city he knew probably better than the back of his hand, he asked: "So where did you go to law school?" I was stunned. So often in law school, our grades are emphasized, as if we'll never get hired anywhere if we don't have decent grades. Not only did Ed not know my grades, but he also didn't even know I had attended Seattle U. He trusted Jackie in selecting me. He gave me a chance.

Ed became more like a second dad to me than anyone. After getting his help or helping him do something on his computer, I frequently just listened to his stories instead of going back to my office to work. He played bad cop to my good cop, and we got things done. My aversion to letting down the façade and exposing my vulnerability to my parents somehow transferred to my inability to reach out to him. He was more compassionate, but imagining myself finally breaking down and sobbing to him and his fabulous wife as I told the story was too much. I still haven't seen or spoken with him since the Last Supper, but I know I will.

Mom

I hardly spoke with Mom during this time, except for the instances I already described. She seemed to be on Team Dad, and regardless of whether her initial suspicion that it was the prescription drugs was right, I assumed she ended up with Dad after the diagnosis. I was now bipolar and needed to be drugged to maintain stability. I feared her because the feeling of *"I want my mom"* would have led me to a totally tearful and sobbing breakdown, which, as a child, I only did with my gray stuffed elephant. To me, Mom wasn't the compassionate comforter I felt safe being vulnerable with. Instead, I saw her and her opinion as threatening to the preservation of my quickly disintegrating nuclear family of two, soon to be one, regardless of my every effort, hope, or prayer. I had come to believe that someone who chose to love and marry me loved me more genuinely. He didn't love me because he had to because of blood, and therefore, he was someone I wanted and valued more in my life than anyone else.

At one point, she did tell me that an investigator called their house. She answered, and when he asked about my location and JD's, she ratted on us. *"She was in a severe car accident and isn't even working, and he lives in West Seattle somewhere. Good luck."* As Ben, who had become my regular driver because of my immobile leg, drove, I held my phone away from my ear for a few seconds, pissed she'd given any information and wondering how to get her to agree not to do it again. I was glad to know to watch out for collections or repossession, guys, though, because I hadn't been paying on my Infiniti and figured they would be closing in soon. Mom didn't wait and threw in, "We've been paying your student loan that's in our names and want you to take that back over soon."That snapped me back to more anger because part of the reason I wasn't working was because of them tricking me into signing into the first mental ward.

"Stop talking to investigators; don't give them any information. And since I'm not working, about the student loan, don't hold your breath," I said, then hung up.

Mom used to be cool. She would take me out of high school if my grades were perfect to go skiing with her on Fridays. Or she would write me notes out of school to ride my horse. Or she would let us open one present Christmas Eve that Dad didn't know about. She could be sneaky. As kids, she told each of us in secret, *"You're my favorite, but you can't tell."* Once, in an argument, my sister had nowhere else to go and pulled her trump card, *"Oh yeah? Well, I'm Mom's favorite!"* My brother and I were silenced and stunned because we thought we were her favorites. I don't remember how she handled the three of us storming up to call her out, but she found a way. Mom used to be crafty, too. I loved helping her make decorative wreaths of cornstalks or pinecones. She sewed us custom comforters with designs of our favorite Care Bears. As our 4-H Club's leader, she helped paint all the *"Seahorse Equestrians"* signage we needed to decorate our club's horse stalls at the fairgrounds. She later dreamed of her own radio show helping people communicate with their animals, like a female Cesar Millan. Over the years, though, these sides of her gave way, seeming to yield to behavior that would reflect well on Dad's image in the community.

Dad

Over the years, Dad and I had some conversations that stood out in my memory. I wish I could forget the first thing he said when I unburdened my heart with the naked truth of my divorce. The last thing I hoped to hear was him telling me the salvation of my soul was his primary concern, and I was going to hell. It may still be the number one thing I wish I had never heard.

Dad's first one-on-one with me was when I was in fourth grade. Report cards just came out, and I knew mine was good. He sat me down, and at six-foot-five, he towered over me even when sitting on the couch, where we watched the *Cosby Show* together. He looked down at me, my report card in his hand. *"Can you explain this B+? You have all A's, but what happened here in Religion?"* I was silent as shock and shame rippled through me. There seemed to be no right answer. How could I explain what I thought was good when he was telling me the truth, which was bad?

My world flipped over. He continued, *"Getting a B+ is not your best, and you're expected to do your best."* My throat tightened as I tried to hold back my tears until I could get to my room. *"Can you do your best from now on?"* he prodded. I meekly nodded and took his hugging me even though I wanted to disappear or teleport directly into my room. From that day forward, I got all A's. When I got an A- in AP History in high school, I resorted to cheating. I had a very methodical way of always coming in later than my friends so I could sit behind them. They studied meticulously, so I was sure to copy most of their right answers while missing the odd one, allowing me to get an A but also differentiating my answers from theirs. I had to seem to do a bit worse because they knew I studied less. It was perfect because they never would have suspected me to be a cheater. I eventually got to spend my senior year of high school as an exchange student in Australia, where all my classes transferred back as pass/fail, having no effect on my GPA. There, I lived free at last, but achieving freedom required me to go 10,000 miles away and not look back. I didn't even know the face of the person picking me up at the airport. It was a little scary, but I was in love with Australia, and the opportunity for freedom was worth surpassing all fear.

Shortly before I left for Australia, Mom and Dad made us go on a family trip to Whistler, British Columbia. Everyone was packed into Mom's blue Suburban. All I wanted was to spend more time with my friends before I left. I was regularly required to spend time with my family for TV nights and Sunday dinners, and I didn't want more of it. I was the reason for the Whistler trip, though. Since we wouldn't be together for twelve months, this was a big deal to Mom and Dad. Dad kept everyone waiting and made me come into his den with him for a talk. I never knew what all went on in the den. I assumed he and Mom talked business, worked out disputes, and made unified decisions about our requests. However, since those conversations always happened behind closed doors, I was never sure.

We sat on his blue leather couch, tufted with metal buttons. To me, it always looked like a psychiatrist's couch but with arms on both ends. It was midsummer because I left for Australia on

July 14, 1994. Wenatchee has a desert-like heat in the summers, often over 100 degrees Fahrenheit. The hot sun burned through the blinds on French doors that led out to his end of the house's back deck. The white-hot light fought the air conditioning, making his couch the coolest place in the room. I sat closer to the door, and slightly backlit, he began his soliloquy. He'd obviously either practiced it or mentally pre-written it. His voice was a little shaky as he got as close to a vulnerable sharing of feelings as he was capable. Letting go of me wasn't easy for him.

"You're like a butterfly," he began. *"I could put a glass cover over you, but I know you would wither away. So, I am letting you go so you can be colorful and free."* He had the *"home court"* advantage in his den, but this wasn't an argument; it was a metaphorical lifting of the glass cover that part of him wanted to keep over me. I took in his words, probably voicing gratitude for the freedom. We both got a little teary and shared a hug while around the room; the walls of his den were dappled with his successes and painted with ethereal and unmistakable pride. His high school diploma, their marriage certificate. A courtroom watercolor. His campaign sign. His face. His father's portrait, smoking a cigarette with a slightly sly smile. The framed print of Wrigley Field. The biggest chair in the room was his, and he lived at the built-in white desk with a rainbow of bookshelves above. They were packed with fiction and nonfiction stories of saints, presidents, and law. Legal legends displayed for fighting for justice and achieving success. The faint yet permanent whisper of his cologne hung in the air, making it seem like he was always there. The built-in desk, white woodwork against the plaid blue wallpaper and custom, two-toned blue carpet were all chosen by him. And it was as if my choice to live 10,000 miles away for twelve months was really his choice to free me.

From freedom, I returned straight away back on the predetermined path to success that my parents set for us. They told us they would pay for college only if we went straight out of high school, and we had to go straight through without stopping. I chose Gonzaga to get in one more year studying abroad, as they had a campus in Florence, Italy, which was the favorite city in the world of most Australians I met. Back in Spokane from the year in Florence and beginning my senior year, it was time to decide what was next. I was sitting on my bed in my upstairs room in the yellow house I shared with four other girls who had been in Italy with me. My blanket was covered in a light blue checkered cover. I'd begged Mom to sew together for me out of two flat sheets. The sun shone through my bedroom window. As I perused two-year graduate programs, I got a phone call. A roommate yelled up to me to get the phone, and it was my dad. I told him what I was up to. His immediate response was, *"You should go to law school; you would be really good at it."*

"Really?!" I asked because I hadn't considered it prior to that call and his firm suggestion. After some discussion and his unwavering support of the idea, I finally gave up.

"I'll go, but if I hate it, I'll quit," I was sure to tell him, so I had an open escape hatch in the event it totally sucked. I convinced myself that a law degree would be like a weapon, and it would give me the ability to provide a six-figure income for my future family if anything happened to my future spouse. I also talked myself further into it when I wrote my law school application essays. I wrote that by becoming a lawyer, I could help make things *"fair"*—I'd never been satisfied when my parents would simply state, *"Life's not fair."* They said it all the time to avoid debate and made it seem like it was something to accept, not to remedy. Without tuning into what really resonated with my heart, my head took the lead, and I did what I thought I should do. I went to law school and then had to start practicing. I couldn't hide my *"light"* because I knew I had to learn how to use it.

Years later, in therapy, is when Dad's next unforgettable words were spoken. I invited him and Mom to one of my appointments with Kari sometime in January 2011. JD also attended that session in silent support and witnessed the dysfunction of my relationship with my parents. Kari's yellow-walled office glowed warmly, and I was a little uncomfortable at the close quarters, which made us sit a little too close for comfort. At one point, Dad shared, *"I have emotions. I just choose not to express them."*

Kari instantly responded, *"Okay, is that a good or a bad thing?"* She quickly corrected herself, *"Do you think that's healthy or unhealthy?"*

Expectations, judgment, reputation, appearances, and Catholicism swirled around the room, leaving me almost suffocated. Like a trip to the dentist without Valium, my discomfort made them uneasy and confused. They denied I could ever feel that way about them. I hardly shared, stunned at his next revelation. Dad got choked up and even started crying. I can easily count on one hand how many times I'd seen him cry. *"I'm scared that next, you'll get depressed, and I'll lose you by you committing suicide."* There it was—his greatest fear. No one could convince him otherwise, least of all me.

At school in Australia, my Aussie classmates often had D&M's. That's short for "deep and meaningful," a conversation necessary to show concern for a friend. They're when we would share support, sort out differences, or just spend a little quality time together. After that, things were water under the bridge, and relationships were frequently made stronger, buttressed by more D&Ms. I've never had a real D&M with Dad.

Chapter 17

THE SHOWDOWN AT THE NORDSTROM CORRAL

Ben took me back to the house to get more of my things. While I was inside, JD got into the car with Ben to threaten him as well. When Ben didn't seem to feel threatened by JD, he instead threatened that he would have to watch out for me, that I was a lawyer, and would come after Ben myself if he tried anything. I left Teddy with JD, believing he needed him more.

Nothing was right, and everything was still a mess, my life in shreds. I hung out with Ben until my money started running low. We visited his grandparents in Oregon, but because of all the anxiety, my inability to sleep continued, and I got worse again. I was almost like a meth head after not sleeping in over a week. Ben did his best to keep up with me, and just staying with me was a miracle. He cared and was there. Overnight, he had become my person. I felt like I was suffering a whole new breakdown because of the death threat, the brutal reality of divorce, my family seeing me as 'crazy Sarah on another manic bipolar trip,' and my grandma still dying of cancer.

At one point, probably around 3 a.m., Ben and I fought and temporarily separated. I walked away, and he drove off. I was barefoot and somewhere near Lake Union. I wandered around like a tweaker. I climbed into an abandoned building and moved some of the old furniture around, envisioning it could be an animal rescue of sorts or it could be the "front" business for our secret missions of helping people. A bit bored, I found a brick and used it to write notes to Ben on the side of the building. I tried to write them so only he would know what they said and that they were for him, from me.

I noticed the glass of a window already cracked. I decided to take my brick to it to get out some anger and see what would happen, how easy it would be to break. I hit it lightly at first, then more forcefully. The glass loudly shattered and then fell to the street, smashing into smaller pieces as it met the pavement. I got scared at the loud sound of the breaking glass and hid. I wondered if the police would come. They didn't, so I kept smashing. It was fun. It became a release for my temporary anger at Ben for whatever reason he couldn't keep up with and understand me, and my bigger anger at my parents. Window after window smashed to the sidewalk. Then I hopped down and silently walked away without cutting my feet, wondering when my mess would be discovered.

Eventually, I wanted to find Ben. I saw some utility workers who had left a giant 1.5-ton pickup running. I tried to jump into their truck to *"borrow it"* to drive around and look for Ben. One of the guys noticed me and, like the Viking years ago, easily grabbed me out of the truck picking me up. I freed myself and got away, yelling obscenities back at him. Now, I'm grateful he kept me from committing a felony. Next, I found a way to cut my finger. Ben had threatened to commit himself because I was making him feel crazy. In my sorely sleep-deprived mind, I wanted to see if he had. But I didn't want to walk barefoot uphill all the way to the hospitals to ask if his name was on record at any of them. To get up there more easily, I knocked on the door of an ambulance sitting on standby in a parking lot. I planned to get a ride and got one. They took me to Harborview Hospital. I asked, but they told me Ben wasn't there. I got a bandage for my finger and maybe a tetanus shot, and before I knew it, they were processing me for a mental evaluation. I believed it was just the next test. One more time, I had to be subjected to inhumane treatment to show them, somehow, what they were really doing to people. My ability to undergo this test showed my inner peace and strength and made me the perfect candidate for the secret group disguised publicly as the Jesuits. Surely, next, I would join the Jesuit Volunteer Corps, which I had applied to join for real a year or so prior. While waiting for the mental health professional to come, I was evaluated as a flight risk. I was probably not agreeing to stay in bed. They ended up cuffing my wrists to the bed. Because I was cuffed, they didn't pay close attention. I stayed calm and assessed the nature of the Velcro-like restraints. I slowly released myself from the restraints, which worked like Chinese finger traps. Resisting them made them tighter, but working my fingers backward through the Velcro was the way to undo them. That late at night, there's not much staff around. I acted casually, got off the bed, went over to the counter, and found my sweater. But I didn't see my pants. Or my underwear. I felt past the point of no return in my escape plan, though. I went to the closest bathroom and quickly shed the hospital gown. I slipped the sweater over my head and looked in the mirror. This would only work if I could make the sweater look like a complete outfit. I splashed water on my face, then ripped the hospital band off my arm and threw it away. I stretched and stretched the black and cream sweater out. It had a huge neck roll that I could put over my shoulders to help make it longer. Sure enough, it could pass for a dress, but I wished I had underwear. The only way out was to leave the bathroom, so I flushed and opened the door. My cover was a barefoot party girl. I figured it must be common with Seattle University's campus only a few blocks away. I walked past the nurses' station, got into an elevator, and made it outside. While I was about to cross the street, one of the staff who must have put it all together came after me. I don't remember what he said. I kept moving. When he stopped following, I realized he could do nothing. I was free, and I knew it. I made my way to the Vintage Park to see if Ben had already moved our things out of that hotel. He had, and we'd left nothing behind. I asked them where I might find free clothes, and they pointed me to a women's shelter a couple blocks away.

I found the shelter, told them the story of JD threatening my life, and made it seem I had nothing. At that moment, I did have nothing. They brought out a few bags of clothes, but they were all awful. I couldn't bring myself to take them. Instead, I asked to borrow the phone and called Jennah. She would have jeans. And flip-flops, too. She agreed to meet me down at Pacific Place. I was getting my hair washed because I could pay for it with the things on hold at Nordstrom if I had to. Instead, she paid for my hair washing, and as soon as she got there, I threw on the jeans and flip-flops she had brought. I might have shared how I got there, and she seemed to remain calm. She followed me around while I killed time, waiting until I had arranged to meet Ben. I think I texted him with her phone and arranged for a reservation at the Westin. He and I had stayed there once before and it was fun, especially having our own beds because he moved a lot in his sleep. But what I didn't know was that she had called my parents and told them my location.

My parents found me and started following me around. They followed me to the bank, walking in the street as I freaked them out worse. My antics were partly on purpose, to scare them away from me, and partly not. I didn't have my ID or a debit card when I went into Wells Fargo, and Dad said, *"You can't get any money out without at least an ID."* I showed him, and the teller who'd met me several times before let me make a small withdrawal and said I could bring my wallet in next time. No matter what I did, though, they followed me. Again, all I wanted was for them to leave me alone, but I couldn't figure out how to make that happen.

I started getting even more tired trying to lose them, and then I got a little creative. I told them, in my sleep-deprived desperation, what I stupidly thought would finally free me of them. I never had any intention of harming myself or anyone else, and I never attempted to do so. But I told them, *"You're going to hear that I'm dead. Don't worry, though. Really, I will be alive and far away, living a new life—without you."* Exasperated, I couldn't figure out any other way to escape. I preferred they think of me as dead so that I could finally just be somewhere new and safe and away. I wanted to create my personal witness protection program to save me from the ground zero that my life had become. Instead, my dad's worst fears seemed to become real. My parents followed me into the Seattle downtown Nordstrom flagship store, where I had planned to meet up with Ben later so we could move our things into the Westin. I went upstairs, temporarily out of their sight. Thinking the coast was clear, I went back down to the store's street-level floor to find Ben. I had bought a couple of things while I was upstairs and was wearing them. Since I had no apparent means to buy them, Mom thought I'd stolen them. What I had done was return what I was wearing for new clothes, a perfectly legal exchange. The supposed suicide threat and their having learned from Jennah that I had escaped Harborview's mental health processing meant they were going to make sure I was returned and caged. They wanted to prevent me from hurting myself, to keep from losing me. They called the police. My mom physically cornered me in the store, refusing to let me go. I tried asking store security for help, saying I didn't know these people. Instead, they were already on my parents' side. I had to abandon the things I'd "pre-bought" and place them on hold so that I could later use or return them if I needed the cash. I had bought rings and a couple of handbags that I wanted to use for my future real wedding to Ben. Sensing security wasn't going to protect me, I headed down the small set of stairs and out the store's west exit. Instead of freedom, I ran into the police, who handcuffed me while an ambulance was on its way. I tried sticking to my story with the paramedics, that I didn't know those people who'd called the police, and I just looked like their daughter. I was from Oregon, I claimed, and they were scaring the shit out of me. Like Belle's father, I was ambushed and carted away in the ambulance. They took me up the hill, and, against every protest, I was caged at Harborview.

Chapter 18

POWERLESS, HELPLESS, AND ALONE

If sharing lessens the pain of something, then here's my biggest share. Because I'm done with the pain. I'm grateful to the page and to you, reader, for being vessels of trust.

Upon arriving at the Harborview, I was at first kept in a kind of holding room, which I was not allowed to leave. The door was locked. Every time I tried opening it, the handle remained stiffly closed. I was free to move about the room but not to open the door. I could overhear in other rooms what I thought were my parents being interviewed about my condition. I secretly hoped they were being told that I was being taken far away or that I was dead. I still held out hope that this was the final process of being accepted into the 'secret program' that would extract me from my life and send me to a life of higher purpose, wherein all my family and friend ties would need to appear totally severed. This was what sleep deprivation and an imagination came up with. They had to give me something because I was again at a total loss for how to cope with my parents just having caused me to be handcuffed and carted away in an ambulance, like a witch on her way to her burning. I had tried denying my identity as if I wasn't their daughter. They were worried about someone else, I said, because I knew they wanted me committed and drugged, and I didn't know how to survive that again. I was still recovering from the first time.

As part of the denial of my own identity, I let the fantasy reality I'd dreamt wash over me. I almost looked forward to the door opening, as if I'd finally be treated humanely and escorted to my new life, which would be like witness protection but better because my ability to survive such terrors made me an asset for whatever cause I was about to join. To confirm my change of identity, I took off my very expensive glasses and twisted the metal of the frames into metal origami, throwing them into the trash. As if, hah, now I can't be identified by my glasses. But this plan backfired, as I also couldn't see more than six inches past my face.

Not being able to see made everything a little bit scarier. But I was committed to my alternate story, desperate for its chance to save me. Of course, my father, being a judge, there was little to no chance of freedom until a court hearing. What contributed to this outcome wasn't just that, though. It was my apparent state of total decompensation, which was scaring the shit out of people who had not only never seen that before but who had certainly never seen it in me. Not to mention my unending and utter fear that my parents would do exactly what they had set out to do time and again like they would not be satisfied, and I would never be totally free until undergoing their answer to my distress:

Commit her!

Commit her!!

Commit her!!!

This was my special form of crucifixion, death by betrayal. Betrayed by my body, heart, and soul's inability to process betrayal. Betrayal by my entire inner circle: husband, best friend, and parents.

I awaited freedom from the holding cell. Alone and confused, all I could do was wait. Relieved to be out of the handcuffs, at least.

But that was temporary. The next thing I remember was being forced to change into hospital clothes, pants, and a top that looked like scrubs but the inmate version. And like an inmate, my next phase of *"processing"* happened to be the one that is my darkest moment.

I was back at Harborview, where they knew I had just escaped after having been tied to a bed by one set of restraints. So they took extra precautions with me beyond just locking me in a padded room. Cruel and unusual punishment, I thought, was totally illegal. I thought even in extreme cases of interrogation of suspected terrorists, the general population believes it to be wrong. Not okay.

I hadn't even committed a crime. Not one that anyone knew about, anyway. In full inmate dress, I was then double handcuffed to a bed. The cuffs weren't metal; they were wrapped in Velcro, as I'd experienced before, so that they could be tighter against your skin than metal. Resisting them caused abrasions on my skin. Because there were two sets, on my ankles and each wrist, there was no getting free. I was good, but I was no magician. My talent was the single Velcro restraint, which was easy to undo once you realized resistance was what kept you in. The way out was counterintuitive. I'm still a tiny bit amazed that I'd figured that out, even in my most messed-up state. Only I hadn't run far enough away because I was still within my parents' reach. My life was still in my father's *"jurisdiction."* No wonder I always felt, and still do feel, most free and most alive and most myself when an entire ocean is part of the physical distance between us.

Even though it hurt, I had to try moving. The people who'd put me into the restraints were gone, and if I could free myself from the restraints, I hoped I'd have a chance at escape when the door opened to me. At least, that was, to me, the only option. I tried and tried, more calmly, to get through one restraint but made little headway.

As I forcefully pulled against the restraints in utter frustration, I heard the chains. Not the clink of the small ones tying my restraints to the bed but the clanging of larger ones. I discovered my bed was chained to the wall. What kind of fucking place was this? I jerked against the restraints again, causing more burns to my arms and lower legs, and realized that the bed was chained to the wall in two places. This made the prior assault and bruises look like a picnic. This was straight-up insane asylum stuff. I was scared shitless. I began to panic. A little stress or anxiety is for babies; this was real shit. Neither of my calming friends, Valium or lorazepam, was there to help me, nor was anyone else.

I was on my period, so not having been given underwear, I knew there would be some blood on my baby blue pants. I shimmied them down, not to expose myself, but to expose the blood, as if where I discovered it might be questioned whether anyone had just sexually assaulted me. This got attention but resulted in my pants being pulled up by strangers' hands. Strangers who were just doing their job. Doing their job meant observing a desperate, fearful woman pull against restraints until her arms and legs were swollen and red. Doing their job meant pulling my pants back up, reporting in my medical records how crazy I was behaving, and leaving me alone for God knows how long.

I'll never know how long I was left like that. Part of me wonders if it was documented in my medical records. Part of me used to fantasize that I could present a case study to a room full of psychiatrists about what it's like to be inhumanely treated. So degraded. So in need of something as simple as a hug but instead locked away, restrained, and caged worse than the worst circus or zoo animal. I felt like an abused animal. I had no civil liberties, no physical freedom.

I was so afraid that I got totally desperate. Once again, Plan A hadn't worked, so it was time to come up with Plan B. For me, that meant I kept pulling at the restraints enough to shake the bed toward and against the wall, letting all the metal clang and bang together so that someone, some nurse, some intern, someone might feel something. Might feel called to help in any way other than what I was experiencing. But I assume that is the current acceptable standard of care for people totally breaking down.

That is what we do to people suffering breakdowns.

Double-cuff them to a bed chained to a wall in a locked room with no windows and cement walls. Leave them alone to scream and cry out for help, and then don't respond.

After the clanging and banging of the bed solicited no response, I resorted to Plan C and added screaming. I screamed out at first with my lungs.

"HELP!!!

SOMEBODY PLEASE.

PLEASE!!!

PLEASE HELP ME!!"

Over and over and over and over. Then nothing. Just the tiniest echo of the chains and screams made their way back to my ears. I was the tree in the forest, and no one could hear me fall. I couldn't even hear anyone traveling the hallway outside my door. I dug deeper. I screamed out from the depths of my soul. Screams a brutally tortured person might make. Worse screams than I'd heard in any movie or television show.

I screamed myself hoarse but never gave up until sheer exhaustion set in. At some point, like the times when I'd blacked out from having drank too much only a few times in the past, I took my last conscious breath and let go. Broken. I died in that room.

Unconscious, I must have been easy to handle because I next remember waking up in a new cell, one in a ward with other inmates. But none of us had committed any crimes. Even the ones who had attempted suicide weren't criminals because it's not a crime to commit suicide. They hadn't been successful because they were here with me, and I'm sure it's not a crime to try. Most people call it an extreme *"cry for help."* I cried, too, but only after *"help"* was being administered.

The answer to the cry is to be locked up. And drugged against your will. Even though you haven't committed a crime or had your day in court. No case has been proven against you for anything; no burden of proof had been met wherein you could defend yourself and cross-examine your accusers. Within three days, you're allowed a hearing about a fourteen-day hold, and you get a public defender who's just doing his job, and there's a light burden of proof. To lock up criminals, we require a burden beyond a reasonable doubt that they committed a crime. I was crimeless but locked up all the same. But it was worse to me because we could be drugged against our will.

I was in a total head haze, hardly remembering whether I slept or ate or when I was dressed; how to open the weird bathroom door that didn't allow me to lock myself in? I had no privacy and no place to find solace unless asleep. I did get sleep because I was given a new friend, Zyprexa, who might as well have been a horse tranquilizer. If they were trying to force normal behavior out of me through prescription drugs, then it might have been easier if I were able to stay conscious and remember something.

Every time I was given a pill in the beginning, I would ask, do I have to take this? Nurse: *"Yes."* *"What would happen if I refused?"* Nurse: *"Then we'll give you a shot containing more than double the dose. Or, we'll, at some point, start electric shock therapy on you."*

Got it. I took the pills. But I don't remember much at all. I was in the more severe ward, and some people had legitimate psychiatric issues. I felt I was being given the exact opposite help that my adjustment disorder required, and I went home suffering some post-traumatic stress disorder from the *"help"* itself. Later, my therapist said I should have been traumatized—I wasn't even supposed to be there.

The others had bandages, wrists usually. Or they were disheveled and unwashed and had such dazed looks they walked the halls like a zombie apocalypse. Creepy as that was, there was again no escape. Just one set of double doors that were the obvious way out, and I wasn't up for another *"door challenge."* I remember how that worked out the last time.

My parents came to visit in the bad ward with my brother and sister before I was allowed a hearing. They were to testify and be at the hearing, so I tried somewhat explaining how I used Nordstrom as a bank and had more money than they realized if I got out and a chance to return the items I'd saved. They thought Ben had stolen or would steal all my stuff, so I'm sure this just reconfirmed for them how messed up I was as they continued to see me through a bipolar filter.

It was disgusting having to be in the bad ward. I didn't want to touch anything. I didn't want to eat anything. There were hardly any clocks or mirrors. Almost like being in a casino. But you're supposed to behave normally in a totally bizarre, fucked-up situation to advance to the less severe ward, where you can eventually earn temporary privileges like a ten-minute meeting with family outside in the fresh air. Eventually, you could return home, vowing to take your medicine to avoid a return. That was the game. The rules were to do whatever the nurses and doctors say and take whatever poison apple they give you, happily, naively, and willingly accepting it into your body, where it would alter your mind and numb your soul. When I tried, on the down-low, successfully advising some fellow inmates on how to get home, I was confined to my room and not allowed to speak to others. When I asked for things from my nurse, I was given the rule of only asking for things on alternating hours. On alternating half-hours, I was allowed out of my room. The rules also changed, like the hypotheticals in law school used to teach us via the Socratic method, like the facts just when you worked out how to maneuver along them.

This wasn't my first time on the inside, but it was the most severely I'd been physically harmed and drugged since the arm bruising and shot. My wrists and ankles were still red and scabbed from the double restraints. I don't remember if I let that be visible to my family when they visited. They acted stupidly to me; I couldn't bear their presence. Their smiles killed me and strangled my heart. They had freedom, their ability to come, visit me, bring me stupid things like a magazine, see me like a caged animal, and then leave. It was sickening. My brother and sister are both licensed attorneys, and my dad is a judge; none of them seemed to give a passing thought to what it might be like to have been stripped bare of my civil liberties, to have zero freedom, zero autonomy, even less so because I was unable to choose what form of *"medicine"* I was to receive.

I tolerated their visits because I hoped their story would change and they might agree that I go home and not continue in the ward. Of course, that would have been too easy. Within twenty-four hours of my day-three hearing, I didn't have to take the medicine. This was so I, the lucid, supposedly real Sarah, could be present at the hearing. Only twenty-four hours out of the Zyprexa haze, I was cuffed to a wheelchair at my ankles and wrists. Finally, the nurse was apologetic about the supposed necessity of it. I think they're just lazy as if they wouldn't want to chase me if I got away again. They didn't trust me not to run. I didn't trust them because they were able to drug me and hold me captive against my will. In my head, that was kidnapping, or at least false imprisonment coupled with assault.

As I was wheeled through the nicer, professionally decorated hallways into an elevator and down to the level of the court, all while chained to the wheelchair, I made small talk with my escort.

We arrived at the court, and Ben was there. I had only a few minutes with my attorney in advance, and I don't remember what was discussed. He probably told me my rights and the process, and I told him I was an attorney, so he shouldn't fuck with me. I had every intention of getting out and caring for myself ASAP.

In the courtroom, the judge entered, and everyone but me stood. I was handcuffed to the chair. I'd stood for the judge to take the bench so many times in my eight years practicing law that it felt alien to be physically restrained from standing. I heard my dad talk about a guy on trial once whose handcuffs were chained to the floor under the counsel's table. The restraints were kept behind a curtain around the table so that the jury could not see and judge him unfairly, as he faced his third strike and would be in jail for life if he lost. I hadn't even committed a crime, and I was restrained with my restraints visible to the judge, in whose hands lay my civil liberties and partial sanity. As the hearing began, the judge immediately recognized my father in the room. She went on the record: *"I see that Judge Small is present in the courtroom. I know him personally, and I'm familiar with him and his occupation on the bench. I'm also aware that you are his daughter. So, if there's any objection to us proceeding today, to me hearing this case, please make it now before we proceed."*

"Yes, I object!" I said, still frustrated at being unable to stand. My attorney, I think putting his right arm across the front of me, said to the court: *"It's okay, Your Honor, we're here now and would like to go forward anyway."*

I could have killed him.

I had to breathe and sit in my handcuffs, ankle cuffs, and wheelchair as I listened to a social worker, a mental health professional, my mother, and my now former best friend testify against me. When I finished my testimony, my lawyer whispered to me that it was the best testimony he'd ever heard. But the judge knew my dad. What the fuck did he think the outcome would be?

I was given fourteen days' hospitalization at Harborview, after which a trial would be scheduled to determine if a ninety-day hold in a mental institution would occur. As soon as the judge failed to recuse herself, I anticipated that outcome but went through the process to preserve a record for an appeal if I could hire a decent private lawyer and represent myself because my public defender was a piece of shit, in my opinion.

I called and complained so much that his supervisor attended the next hearing when the trial date was set. I couldn't get a different lawyer, I was told, and my defender was good at his job and I needed to work with him. I learned there were only two guys in town who did the stuff privately and they each wanted closer to $10,000 cash for their time and to cover a medical evaluation, and one of them was unavailable.

I was fucked. The fourteen days were going to finish out, but I would be damned if the next ninety would occur. My parents wanted that, of course, then for me to come live with them for about six months after that so they could medicate and supervise me themselves. There was no way on earth I would allow that to happen. I tried to call the W, as I was able to look up the hotel's phone number with the internet access I had, and asked for the *"whatever, whenever"* department. Since I couldn't pay my lawyer, I told them I was a former hotel guest and begged them to look up the contact information for an MHP with whom I could schedule a reevaluation so I would have to be released. My interior requests for that were, of course, denied. Once they determined I was not a current guest and totally out of it, they hung up on me, refusing help.

More desperate, and while on Zyprexa, I called the psychiatrist I had worked with, but his office would not cooperate with whatever I was demanding. Frustrated, I fired him. I thought that showed him, but I really showed me because I got absolutely nothing from them after that.

Zyprexa felt like part Mind Eraser, a drink I first had at my friend Beth's wedding, the first wedding of the prior year. I mostly remember the meds making me sleep and making my stay in the worse ward more difficult to remember. They kind of drugged the fight out of me. At least my appearance of succumbing led to a change in prescription to a less severe drug called Seroquel. Zyprexa was gone; substitution, Seroquel. Behavior and drug changes led to my graduating to the less severe ward instead of the freedom I longed for. But the Seroquel was causing me increased blood pressure and physical side effects to the point that they were also trying to make me take heart medication. May I refuse the heart medication? Nurse: *"Yes, but you are suffering side effects." "How long will it take before my heart gives out and I die from the side effects?"* Nurse: *"Ten years." "Well, I don't plan on being here that long, so I'm turning down the heart medication. I want it documented what you're causing to happen to me physically."*

I'm sure it wasn't just the medication's side effects that caused my rise in blood pressure. I was fully and very aware that I officially had no civil liberties. None. I was not able to refuse medication. I was physically still restrained, not by cuffs, but by walls. Out of sheer desperation, even though I was excruciatingly embarrassed to be committed, I reached out to JD. He had promised he would not allow my parents to do that to me again after they had tricked me into signing myself the first time. He promised. I asked him to help get me out of there. He refused. I reminded him of the promise and demanded he help and honor his word, not realizing how futile my request was until I heard his repeated denials. He was through dealing with them. He was through with me, too. I found out that he'd filed for divorce. They tried serving papers, but the servers couldn't get past the security of the ward. I stared at the cars rolling along I-5, longing for free air. Even if it meant sitting in hours of traffic, at least they were free.

I didn't even work toward the privileges of ten minutes outside because that, to me, was not free air. Why play along? I wanted to breathe freedom.

I meditated. I slept. I walked laps around the hallway after everyone went to bed. I probably walked two miles a night with my headphones in, listening to Kid Cudi that Ben had uploaded to my iPhone. I walked so fast around the halls as I pretended to be part of a film crew, there to watch in documentary-like style how bizarre the behavior of not only the patients but also the nurses. I quietly and carefully watched the nurses in the less-severe ward. The last ones, in the bad ward, were very attentive. These, not so much. Like, they trusted us, inmates, a tiny bit more. They assumed when we popped pills into our mouths, took a drink, tilted our heads back, swallowed, and opened our mouths to show emptiness that we were taking medicine. I realized that they didn't watch us after the *"head tilting, mouth opening show."*

There was my window.

About halfway through what ended up being a three-week incarceration but pretrial release under a less-restrictive ninety-day order, I tried what must have been Plan Z.

I'd already stopped asking each time what would happen if I refused the dose, making them say each time that I'd have to be given a shot with double the dose. I had fleshy cheeks and practiced first tucking a bit of food to see if it was visible, and then I went for it. I took the pill, and as I drank and tilted my head back, I tucked it into the bottom of my inner lower cheek. As my head came down, I showed her my swallow. I opened my mouth and showed her my tongue. She smiled and moved on to the next inmate. I sat, watching television for a hot minute, and then casually went to my room to pee. Securing the bathroom door, I quickly scraped out the pill and spit it into the toilet, also peeing for good measure so I could truthfully say I was just going pee and flushed. One small victory for Sarah-kind. I did it. They didn't catch me. Excitement and relief glowed inside me, a secret phoenix rising. It was easier than I anticipated, just go through the motions and repeat that little success. Again, and again, and again. It worked. I was finally coming to. I was finally more me. They began telling me: *"You're doing so well!"* While I tried not bitch-slapping their face in response. They assumed the meds were doing the trick, and I was finally benefiting from their magic. I wanted to shake them silly. I wanted to scream out, *"You are fucking idiots, I'm not taking the fucking medicine!"* Instead, I told my lawyer because he had to keep it in confidence, and I told Sophie, who would not betray me as I felt Jennah had. My other outlet continued to be haiku poetry, which began in the worse ward. For some reason, cramming my feelings into a succinct and simple 5-7-5-syllable block was liberating.

Sobriety from the meds proved to be a double-edged sword because I only more excruciatingly appreciated the fact that I had no civil liberties. I could also clearly see, although as my dad later pointed out in a harsh email that technically the *"State ofWashington"* put me there, that my parents and friend (but officially no longer best friend) had played significant roles.

One of the nicest people I've ever met in law is Jillian White. She had her practice in Seattle, focused on family law and adoptions, but I met her when we were appointed together for the minors in the difficult estate case. When it was time to close my office, she took the King County cases of my biggest client, a professional guardian. I met her in a QFC parking lot to transfer the physical files, and she gave me a big hug. She, like Mike, embodied heart and intellect in her practicing law. She seemed to juggle running her office with being a mom and wife and herself with ease. She was always reachable through her message service, and she was the only lawyer to visit me when I graduated from the less severe ward. I'm sure she brought me chicken pad Thai, and we shared lunch at one of the white metal tables, sitting in the uncomfortable white plastic chairs, eating noodles from foam containers with plastic forks. She knew I shouldn't be there. One more member for Team Sarah. Her one visit was the most normal experience I had while on the inside.

When my dad visited once, I told him I couldn't live in boxes like he did anymore. He was comfortable there, but I couldn't do it. He looked at me through the filter of bipolar, as if I was speaking in tongues. I didn't know how else to convey it, but my way of seeing the world is not how he sees his world. Just like the Dachau gate that said in German that *"work makes you free,"* for my father, rules make him free. My freedom would be found in living outside the boxes, in the spaciousness of simplicity. I had no other way to describe it to him, so I dropped it and moved on to my sketch of circles. One circle contained the toxic people in my life, and another, my new inner circle of trust. To his dismay, he found himself with the toxic branding, and he shook his head in disbelief. I let him leave without assaulting him for having put me there. Still, a small sense of helplessness returned because it felt like there was no way to get through to him while he looked at me that way. At least, not until his Tin Man self grew his own heart. Courage and brains were never his deficit.

When Jennah visited me in the less-severe ward, I asked for an apology. I understood she felt that she had to testify when called, especially as an attorney. But not only had she testified, she had told my parents my location in the first place. She insisted she was only helping me and refused to apologize. I have had to accept that, but I can no longer call her my best friend. In my book, that is not what best friends do. To me, best friends go to the fucking mat and throw down for you. That's Sophie's style.

Chapter 19

RED TO THE RESCUE

My assistant, Sophie, ended up being my main ticket out of Harborview. Hiring her and becoming her friend turned out to have been two of my best decisions. She helped rescue me from the aftermath of what I thought had been my best decisions.

I wanted to hire her as soon as I finished interviewing her. My mom had come over to help me interview assistants. Sophie went first. I was sold. I knew in my gut she was the one. She was experienced and seemed to be made of the stuff that Ed was made of—the real deal and full of integrity. Mom talked me into finishing the other seven interviews and then choosing who had been my second choice for reasons I don't even recall. Second-choice girl lasted one day. One day. I came in on day two to a Post-it Note on the staff computer screen, the office keys left below, saying I didn't even owe her for the one day she came in. She was thinking about leaving another office, and I guess the amount of work to do in mine scared her back there. I called Sophie.

"Please, I need you, please—this girl ran away after one day. I need help! I need your help!" I begged. She laughed. She tried to hang up on me. *"Are you kidding? I never work for someone when I'm their second choice."* I didn't give up, I persisted. We discovered we were

both from Wenatchee. It came up who my dad was. She must have gulped. *"Your dad's law office in Wenatchee was where I got my start in law..."* *"It's payback time,"* I joked, with all seriousness because I was desperate, and she was it. She relented, to the surprise of her and her husband. I struck a chord. I was the kid that my mom used to parade through the office to show the secretaries what they'd be messing with if they messed with him.

While Sophie was working for me at full capacity, she could do the work of two and a half people. But she'd been rear-ended by a drunk driver about a month before my life meltdown, which was partly why she left my office to recover the year prior, once I was out of the institutions. She was still not back to work while I was involuntarily at Harborview, but she was more than willing to help me *"just keep swimming"*—she loves to quote Dory from Finding Nemo, second only to Dr. Seuss's quotes always at the end of her emails. She knew I didn't belong there, and while Ben continued to visit, she did her damn best to help eventually get me home.

To get me home, Sophie helped me show the Harborview medical professionals that the information they gained from my parents was false. Plain and simple. They thought I'd lost my house in foreclosure had no car, no job, and no money. All incorrect. One by one, we proved by calling my bank that my house was not in foreclosure, by calling my work that my paychecks had been mailed, and I was welcome to return anytime, and so on. It was daunting because each time the doctors changed shifts, the newest one had to get on board. Ultimately, Kari had to convince the doctors that my family was a source of stress and not to involve them. The staff couldn't conceive of an educated, upper-class family like ours being my worst nightmare instead of my greatest supporter.

Home. I finally found out that Grandma died, and her memorial was while I was in Harborview. They didn't want to tell me and upset me. As if I could have been more upset than I was to be caged, without my civil liberties, and drugged against my will. She was gone, and I didn't get to say goodbye. I only felt more adrift at losing her, too. I knew I needed more time to grieve but would need to work again soon to support myself.

I gave myself about two weeks to chill out and then went back to work at the dealership, where my general manager, Bob, welcomed me back with open arms and a big hug. He'd talked to me throughout the ordeal and had a *"so what"* attitude. Everybody has their shit, he'd say, and it was okay. I guess a lot goes down in the car business. I was glad to be somewhere I wasn't judged for it and got to stick around if I sold cars.

I let Ben move into the house with me, and it was nice not to be alone anymore. By August, he found some work selling subscriptions to the News Tribune, then instead got hired to work at Little Caesars, mostly as a sign dancer, which he loved. It felt like I had somewhat accidentally gotten into what was transparently a rebound relationship, and within a few months or so of being home, I knew I had to end it. I wasn't ready for something like that with anyone. I needed some time on my own and needed to get it on with a green-eyed soldier I had just sold two trucks to. It was difficult and sad to end it with Ben, but at the same time, he ended up staying at the house instead of becoming my live-in toy boy. He had been there for me in unimaginable ways, and I wouldn't kick him to the curb. He earned his keep as a house bitch. For cigarettes or a bowl, he'd happily be down for car washing, vacuuming, dishes, cooking, laundry, dog walking, taking the trash out, mowing the lawn… and, of course, the occasional fun still went on. I'm glad that I realized it was ridiculous for me to attempt any type of relationship, given my life and my heart were in shreds.

I saw my parents every few weeks so they could see me acting normally, for fear that they would try something else like guardianship if they didn't. I would have Ben go with me to meet them for lunch or dinner. It was usually awkward, and I felt fake. Whenever I left for the bathroom, they would ask Ben, *"Is she taking the medicine?""Yes, she is,"* he appeased them, as we agreed he would. He would fill me in later. They never asked me if I was taking the medicine. They wanted to know if I would stay stable, and they thought that the medicine was the way that would happen.

I let Dad take me to a birthday dinner in December 2011, after I got off work. He met me at the dealership, and I introduced him to everyone, taking him on a quick drive in a new Jeep Grand Cherokee. I was scared to leave work, where I'd really be alone with him at dinner. I had him take me to Paddy Coyne's, which reminded me of Fiddler's Elbow, the Irish bar in Florence where I'd studied almost daily years ago. He sang to me and gave me a present like I was a kid. I sucked it up, not enjoying it but going through the motions for him, and still partly to protect me from him trying something again that was designed to help me but instead hurt me. The present was $50 cash, and he apologized it couldn't be more. I didn't care. Before the present opening and singing, he'd asked me about my divorce. JD had filed for divorce while I was still in Harborview. I had hired an attorney, and we were still negotiating, but my dad believed otherwise. *"Your attorney hasn't filed anything, and for all you know, it's over, and a default was entered against you,"* he accused. I was speechless. I just took out my iPhone, logged into Linx (the local county online records system), and showed him all the filings that were in order. *"What about these?!"* I showed him.

"Oh. Well, SCOMIS [the statewide court records system) doesn't show that." He moved on after that, and I left him without an apology. Next, I got to hear, *"How can you live with yourself morally, selling cars?"* I explained that banks only approve what someone's income

supports that they bet on interest income, not people failing their obligations. He didn't seem sold. I gave up. I survived the dinner that pretty much ruined my birthday, silently vowing not to subject myself to this again, especially not on another birthday. I hardly met up with my parents for meals after that, preferring to leave them guessing about my condition rather than subject myself to more of that.

Chapter 20

THE CRASH

December of 2011 was my best month in car sales. I earned a commission check of around $12,000 gross that month. I was elated. If only I had known before law school that something like selling cars would be so much fun for me and pay well at the same time. I could do it, and with effort, I was doing it even better. I felt like things, life in general, were getting back on track. I felt like I was finally getting on my feet. I was on the other side of my divine storm. I wasn't sure what was next, but I wasn't caring too much either. I was going through the motions while still going through the grieving process at the same time. I was slowly feeling better about things in general. I figured the more time that went on without mental health incidents, the better I could prove to my family that I was not bipolar, that my psychiatrist's adjustment disorder diagnosis was right, and that I had naturally and fully recovered.

It was a Saturday night, so the dealership closed early, at 8 instead of 9. February 11, 2012, I got off work and drove my little '92 Plymouth Laser to get cheap Chinese takeout, about ten minutes up the road from my house in Sumner. I had been driving the Laser, keeping the Infiniti out of sight until I figured out what to do with it or if it was possible to negotiate with my bank. I went for takeout partly to avoid going home because Ben and I had fought via text messages that day. What about, I have no idea. But I was mad, and instead of confronting him, I took time to cool off and get dinner. I considered seeing a movie, too. I watched a few movie previews on my phone, the steaming orange chicken on the passenger seat next to my peach tea. I could escape our conflict a little longer by seeing a movie. Nothing grabbed me. One freaked me out: the preview for *The Vow*. It was a movie where there was a bad accident, and the girl woke up not remembering that Channing Tatum was her husband. As soon as I saw the crash part of the preview, I freaked and knew there was no way I was down for watching that. Away I drove, apparently to live my own version of it instead of watching.

Boom. Crash. Just like that, in an instant, I was broken. This time, physically.

I barely saw it coming. A 1989 pickup truck, a gross green hunk of metal, pulled out in front of me on the highway. He was turning left to head opposite the direction that I was coming. Moving at what seemed like a snail's pace, he left me nowhere to go. No way out. In the few seconds I had, I tried working out how I might avoid him, but it quickly became obvious that a collision was unavoidable. I accepted, in a matter of seconds, that possibly the last thing I ever saw would be the side of an ugly, green truck. I closed my eyes. As my body flew forward, smashing into the steering wheel, my car crumpled as easily as a hand-held accordion. I heard a thunderous crack of metal on metal. It felt like everything broke at once, me and my car. I had a strange taste in my mouth. Even my teeth were broken.

My gut instincts told me not to make any attempt to get out of the car. I didn't move. Chinese takeout plastered the gray-upholstered insides of the Laser. As I reached for my phone to call

9-1-1, a witness opened my car door. He asked if I was alright. I automatically said no. He let me know help was already on its way. I couldn't see out my smashed windshield because my hood was up, blocking my view. Able to do nothing but wait, I began crying hysterically. Partly in relief because help was coming, but mostly from fear and the pain. I had never broken a bone before, and I later learned that was the main source of my physical pain. While my phone was still in my hands, I wasn't sure at first who to text or call. I'd had a fight with my live-in ex-boyfriend/toy boy, or whatever we were at that point. I'd been too upset to go home right after work. I still don't remember now what the fight was about.

Still in shock, I managed to text Ben. *"I was in an accident... I'm going to a hospital... I don't know which one..."* right before the paramedics took off my big puffy black work coat and inadvertently left it behind, with my wallet and phone inside the pockets. The ambulance ride was no picnic, as it was not my first ambulance rodeo, and being restrained to the backboard was, likewise, not unfamiliar territory. I was torn between physical pain and flashbacks, preferring neither, but once again had no route of escape.

I was taken to the ER, and after being wheeled in while waiting for the doctor and as my head began to get a piercing pain from the backboard that I was taped to, I started to think about who I wanted to contact. No one came to mind. Crickets. I had to contact Ben somehow because I did have to get home one way or another. But I didn't know where we stood. Still, besides him, I didn't feel compelled to reach out to anyone, family or friends, especially not my almost ex-husband. He didn't seem to care much about me or our vows—ever since I learned about his indiscretions with other women in Hong Kong. Prostitutes? Or just a couple of random Australians who I found out later became his 'friends' on Facebook? Come on, like it mattered, really, because that act and actions to follow spoke louder than any words he'd ever promised me.

Unfortunately, Ben had a new number, and the only place I knew I could get it was on JD's tablet. I'd used it before he left on his last trip, and before giving it back to him, Ben insisted on leaving a message in the notes application: *"If you're ever concerned about Sarah, please feel free to contact me, #..."* I didn't know any other close friend's current number by heart, and it was nearing midnight. The last people I wanted rushing to help in person were family, considering what they might discover upon bringing me home—that I'd become a medical marijuana patient. Hah! That was the absolute last controversy I needed to deal with, especially in my newly broken and painful condition. So, I called JD and left a brief message about the accident, saying, *"I'm okay, please call Ben and the hospital..."*

JD, an international cargo pilot and 747 captain, called the Good Samaritan Hospital ER from Colombia, South America. I remember more what he didn't say than what he did say. I could have died, and he didn't even tell me that he loved me. At least he called. By the time he spoke with Ben, Ben had ironically figured out where I was and was already on his way. Score one in his W column. I hung up with JD, feeling like the connection we shared and the entire basis for our marriage may have been my own personal delusion. Did he ever love me, truly love me? Did it even matter? Because it was over. And now I had a freshly broken leg to match the feeling of a still broken heart.

Apparently, a tibial plateau fracture meant that the main bone in the bottom of my leg was shattered at the knee joint, and I learned that it would take one or more plates and about a dozen screws to put it all back together. While a surgeon could repair my leg in a few hours of surgery, I continued to wonder how long it would take to repair my heart.

JD later seemed to come around. We met up, and, over dinner, he said he'd had an *"epiphany"* but offered no other words that left me inclined to reconsider. Other efforts, in the form of things like an iPhone, were gifts that also didn't have the effect he'd hoped for.

I spent one night with him after my leg surgery. He cooked lamb chops. It was okay, like a colored-pencil sketch of what used to be, but the hopelessness of history overshadowed the small hope of something. He deserved a second chance—with someone else, as I think Mae West once said.

Chapter 21

SURGERY, HOSPITAL VISITS, AND FOUR MONTHS COUCHBOUND

The surgery required a four-day hospital stay. Ben drove me there and was with me while I checked in. He was great, kept me smiling, and wheeled me around. He shared with the nurses that he was my toy boy. Hospitals aren't his favorite place either, so he eventually headed home. My mom came in before I was taken away. She was sure to inform the anesthesiologist how I reacted to Ambien, digging right into things I preferred to leave buried. I interrupted her and let her know she could go, I was ok. With a shattered tibia, I couldn't get away, and I just had to lay in the bed and talk her into leaving instead. I was wheeled into the operating room. I had to slide over to another, harder, colder bed. I saw a bunch of metal instruments around the room and iodine stains on the floor. I closed my eyes and waited for the anesthesia to kick in.

I woke up in a hundred times more pain than I had pre-surgery. My leg was huge, and I couldn't move. I woke up every time I could hit the pain button on my IV and let more meds numb me, this time from physical pain. Here I was again, in a hospital and not able to move. Remembering the mental torture while feeling the physical torture. I had visitors again, too. JD came and made a weak offer of assistance, like he could take a few weeks off work to help me. I told him no thanks. I knew he wouldn't take off a whole three to four months and be willing to cater to my every need, that was not his forte. Also, in his next breath, he asked about when our divorce could be finalized because *"What if I meet someone while I'm out walking Teddy?"* Wow, I guessed maybe he already had met someone and just preferred to pursue it after the divorce was final. I knew part of his offer was a move to get Ben out of the house. But there was no one I'd rather have care for me than Ben. He had already done so well leading up to surgery, too. He had a way of making me feel better in my heart, not just of helping me physically get around. He was what I needed more of, and I knew it.

Sophie visited with her twelve-year-old grandson she was raising and brought me a plastic bucket of goodies, filled with crayons and coloring books that reminded me of how my grandma taught us to color. She had a special way of pressing harder along the boundary and lighter to fill in the middle of the blank spaces. She also taught me how to draw a simple rose. Sophie's goodie bucket was thoughtful. She stuck around to chat, too. Even though I was uncomfortable, she took my mind off the pain. My dad also came in while she was there. At that point, my pain went through the roof because of how anxious he made me feel. It was like I was right back in a mental ward with him next to me. I couldn't get away from him, and she noticed my change. She chatted away until he said I must be tired and needed to rest so he would leave. He remarked that she sure talks a lot. He left, and she stayed. I relaxed. She laughed. As soon as he left, I had less pain and felt more up to talk. My parents' *"best"* was still not what I needed. I needed space. I needed people to see me, not see me through the bipolar filter.

My parents offered me a ride home. I made the nurses help me stay one more night, four total, so that they would have to go home to Wenatchee instead, and Ben could drive me home. I later told my dad over via text message that I didn't want them driving me home because we were smoking in the house. (They thought cigarettes, but I was more afraid of them seeing my pipes for weed since I had become a medical marijuana patient for my migraines when it became legal in 2011.) Dad's response was, *"Mom says 1-800-quit-now."* I was fed up. I replied with a suggestion of my own. I let him know that I had listened to their unsolicited advice for over thirty years, and I requested that it stop. Simple request. But his response was, *"You should at least hear my advice and then consider whether you want to follow it or not."* No boundary was respected.

It took a while before I could get around with a walker. I spent months couchbound, pill-popping as often as sixteen times a day, watching hundreds of hours of Netflix, and consuming lots of pizza and weed. Initially, Ben had to lift my leg for me just to get up, go pee, get into the shower, or even put on underwear. I was grateful our past relationship made me comfortable with him assisting me so intimately.

Eventually, I had Ben go with me to one more miserable dinner with my parents before I gave up. I was done pretending I was taking the medicine. I told my dad over email that I wasn't taking the medicine, I was not bipolar, and I hadn't felt like being around them ever since they had me committed. His response was typical. *"We didn't commit you, the State of Washington did, and as a lawyer, you should know that."* It reaffirmed, once again, why I preferred not to stay in contact.

While I recovered, I renegotiated the terms of my divorce, too. I decided I would not worry about money or health care and only focus on healing for at least a year. I decided what I wanted and communicated directly with JD over text. He refused; I held my ground. He gave in. I called my lawyer to relay the terms. My lawyer said he couldn't have gotten what I got for myself and that no court would have given it to me. I knew that. I loved that in the final property award, the first item awarded to the wife was:

Dog, Teddy.

It was tough being stuck on the couch. My first activity was tanning because it was the easiest thing I could do: lay on a bed instead of the couch. I felt better after, so I continued to do it. Next was swimming, before later I finally made it back to hot yoga and then my trainer. I was in no rush to do much but heal, and I dabbled in possibility. Not living from my heart before had led to disaster. Still, I hesitated to dream or commit to new dreams.

Chapter 22

INSURANCE LICENSE

Worrying about what work I would do next, I got anxious. I scanned Craigslist for options. The job listings had led me to cars, and, like a Magic 8 Ball, I hoped they would show me what was next. I found a listing for great paying, work-from-home insurance sales. I would supposedly take inbound calls and sell insurance over the phone, and they would train me how to do it. I had nothing else going on; I was still couchbound, so I easily went through the Washington State training. By the time I was getting around with crutches, I took the state licensing exam. It was cake compared to the bar exam. I passed and got my license. Then, the webinar-style training began. I listened every morning for hours, bored to tears, about the products and sample interactions. I got a bunch of PowerPoint presentations to show people via webinar what I was providing them. I saw the value in the products but not in how I would be fulfilled, never being face-to-face with my customers. I also eventually found out I was expected to pay for my own leads. I was not at all excited to do it, although the opportunity for residual income sounded so good initially. It was paperwork-intensive, too, on the level that I would want to hire staff again. I had been there and done that. I was over it. I felt before that the business owned me more than I owned it, and I was becoming more attached to freedom than anything else. I finished the training and never sold a policy.

Chapter 23

BABY PHOTOGRAPHY

By the time December rolled around, I hadn't worked in almost a year. I got two doctor's notes, one that said I could work part-time, light-duty, and another that said no full-time. I sent the second one to the dealership and scanned Craigslist again. This time, I focused on the part-time jobs section. What fun thing could I get up to? Late one night, I saw an ad for part-time newborn photography at the hospitals that paid commission. The company was called First Moments. I thought it would be a great way to get over my fear of being in hospitals as well as my ache for what seemed to be missing: a new baby that would have been part of my happily ever after that was no longer.

I submitted my resume online, and it then went through an online application process. I was too tired to finish it, so I went to bed. I woke up to a phone message that they loved my resume, would I please do the application? I quickly applied and heard back that afternoon. Noel would be interviewing me and others at a nearby hospital the next day. I knew then that I was already hired. A guy doing the interview. I figured I could look cute and get hired.

I wore a cute dark jean dress and brown knee-high boots from Florence. I walked into the lobby through the hospital's automatic sliding doors. A scattered, thirtysomething guy in a suit but no tie and messy hair was pacing the lobby while on his cell phone. He glanced at me and paused, then went back to his conversation. I smiled. I knew I was hired. He hung up, introduced himself as Noel, and we found the other girls. He spent time with us as a group explaining the job, including the sales aspect of it, and then started the individual interviews, making sure I was last. I waited and waited in the cafeteria. Finally, the second-to-last girl told me it was my turn.

I walked over to the table where Noel sat by the window and sat down. He looked at his notes, then up at me. Before he asked a question, I had one of my own. *"So, I should just show up for training, right?"* He almost spoke, then swallowed and said, *"Yeah, you're hot, and you're hired."* Then he said we should talk a bit more anyway, and he explained his history with the company. He learned a bit about my experience selling cars. He said I would probably quit quickly, but he would take the heat for me, and he asked if I wanted to get a drink. I said yes.

It was so entertaining. We went to a sports bar and ended up making out in the booth, then up against my car. I refused to sleep with him, though, wanting a *Grey's Anatomy* experience only after I was officially hired. Except he ended up getting fired before that happened. Not because of me but other girls complained. In the meantime, I went through all the training and unexpectedly fell in love with taking pictures. It was so different with a professional camera. My pictures, even during training, were good. I started having fun again, even though getting up and down off the floor and handling babies while maneuvering the camera and flash was a little taxing, given my healing leg and body. While I was in elementary school, my mom let me take two *"college for kids"* classes at our town's local community college. I chose photography and creative writing. Along the way, as my parents made me into a *"well-rounded"* and *"straight-A"* student, I forgot to make room for what interested me. Doing what I *"should"* for so long, I forgot there were things I liked loved. Things that, when I do them, I enjoy them so much time ceases to exist. The baby photography might not have been my forever job, but I was glad that I started to really enjoy doing something.

Chapter 24

CHOPRA CENTER

The insurance settlement from the car accident came in the mail sometime in January 2013. I have never seen a check so big and in my name before $100,000. I took a picture. These policy limits were all they had to "make me whole" from the physical pain and suffering accidentally caused by the green truck driver. I was still physically recovering from what my surgeon told me was the slowest-healing injury I could have gotten. My last doctor's notes allowed me to work part-time (baby photography) but not full-time (still off work from selling cars). Physical therapy was over, and I continued swimming. I had started the prior September, and it was the only other activity besides going tanning that felt good. I did my breaststroke, mixed with sidestroke one way and sidestroke the other. Always head above water. I never liked the crawl stroke we were taught as kids in the country club swimming lessons. I feared turning my head to the side to breathe in water instead of a pocket of air that was supposed to be created with each stroke. I swam the way I wanted and let the other LA Gym members have their crawl stroke. Swimming was gently helping me to strengthen my leg and lose weight at the same time. The less weight I carried, the better my leg was also feeling.

In the pool, I meditated. I would pick mantras I'd learned from the twenty-one-day meditation challenges I did with Deepak Chopra online. My favorites were *"so hum,"* which means *"I am."* Sometimes, the simplicity of that one was too boring. I would instead repeat with every two strokes, *"aham brahmasmi,"* which means *"I am the universe."* I liked that one. I could mentally repeat it for an entire hour in the pool, hardly breaking my concentration. It kept me from reliving the worst moments I'd had with JD and my parents in the last year. When I first started swimming, I spent part of the time holding back tears as those repeated frustrations would simmer and boil over in my mind. I would try letting the physical activity wring the hurt out of my soul, but I didn't feel like progress was being made. I switched to my mantras. The other favorite was *"sat-chit-ananda," "truth, consciousness, and bliss."* This one was for the days when I felt most aimless and lost, and in a way, the words returned me to what I preferred to feel life was about.

I followed Deepak on Facebook through his Chopra Center, liking the messages and information about Ayurveda, but also awaiting the next free twenty-four-day challenge. I noticed an announcement for one of their seminars called *"Healing the Heart."* I was drawn to it. I read about it. I wanted to go, but I hesitated. I would need to arrange for someone to cover me for my photography shifts. Then I realized I had time to give two weeks' notice that I was quitting so that upon my return, I could instead pursue whatever I felt was next. The photography shifts were a little physically taxing—my leg wasn't quite up to the challenge. And, besides, I already felt better about being in hospitals. That, and I felt better around babies. All my friends and siblings were having babies. Visiting them was like visiting my lost dreams. I had to get over it. Being in the hospital and around babies helped me heal myself. I was less sensitive from the PTSD I was later diagnosed with from being hospitalized against my will. I was also happier than sad to be around new lives as they were welcomed into growing families.

I thought, why wouldn't I do something that would help heal my heart? I signed up and put in my notice at First Moments. It was just as Noel had predicted; I was quitting just after I'd begun, but I knew it wasn't for me in the long term. The weekend was at the Chopra Center in Carlsbad. My aunt lives nearby, and I was excited to see her. As a Carmelite nun, she told me that anything *"New Age"* is the devil, but she respected my choice to go. I appreciated her willingness to meet me halfway. Ben and I took turns driving, and Teddy took turns in our laps. Ben DJ'd, and we drove all the way to SoCal. It was my first time out of Washington since early 2010. I loved it. So did Teddy and Ben. Sunshine, ocean air, and freedom. We felt renewed.

On the first day of the seminar, I learned *"Primordial Sound Meditation."* It begins with asking three rhetorical questions: Who am I? What do I want? What is my dharma/purpose? Then, we are to let those go unanswered and meditate on our mantra. They all begin with Om and end with Namah. The middle word is the sound that the universe was making when you entered the world. The sound is assigned based on the exact date, time, and location that you were born. It's a sound you're directed not to tell anyone, and it is given to you only by someone trained in such meditation. The sounds of the earth were discovered thousands of years ago by yogis or monks who meditated so long that they became discernable. This became my go-to meditation when I wasn't trying a new one on my Om app, swimming to a mantra, or participating in a yoga class that, for me, was always a moving meditation. I would set my timer and Om ___ Namah myself into inner peace. Sometimes, it was easier to focus than others, but the more I meditated, the easier it was for me to reconnect with a sense of peace in one breath, an ability that had totally escaped me for so long.

The weekend was intense but transformational. I never knew it was possible to feel such compassion from strangers. And I learned all pain is the same. It's universal to the human experience, and no matter how vastly different our experiences were, we all felt the same pain. At the end of the weekend, we did a ceremony at the beach and threw rocks into the ocean. Mine were named Valium, Celexa, lorazepam, etc. It would take longer for me to make peace with, let go, and forgive JD and then Mom and Dad, but I was on my way.

I loved SoCal and wanted to move there. I tried looking for places before we left, but none of them took dogs, or they didn't respond, or they were too expensive. Jennah moved there a couple of months later. Even after getting back home, I considered it. I pushed to test the universe's response. Nothing opened. It felt too soon to move. I had a good situation that was supporting my ability not to work and just heal, so I put that idea on the back burner.

Chapter 25

LULULEMON

By the time March rolled around, I was feeling up to returning to hot yoga. It had been a year since the accident, and I didn't know how long they would really keep my unlimited two months on *"hold"* status. I was sick of swimming, too. I needed something new. I restarted my time and added five additional months for the price of three. It was tough, especially when my right side was so much stronger than my left. One of the instructors let me know only to go as far on my right as my left could go so that I didn't reinforce the unequal strength. I dialed it back on the right side and kept going.

It was so hot, and I would get so sweaty that I decided to invest in clothes that I would be comfortable practicing in. I was going at least five times a week and sometimes to the cartilage-stretching Yin classes, too. I tried some of the brands at the REI or Road Runner Sports near home, then, like Goldilocks not happy with her bed, I found the hot yoga gear that felt *"just right"* at Lululemon.

I became a Lululemon addict. It was the perfect gear for hot yoga, and because it was designed to last over four years of regular use, I saw it as an *"investment"* in my health. Of course, the extra hoodies I first purchased there to wear so I fit in at the Chopra Center were more for comfort and fashion than for yoga. Just shopping there was an experience because everyone was so nice. And they were all into yoga, like me.

One afternoon at the University Village Lululemon, Thomas invited me to apply to work there. I must have seemed like I would fit in. After some coaxing, he let me know if I did apply to be sure to go on their website and, download the goal-setting worksheet, fill it out, and submit it with my resume. I went home, perused their whole website, watched YouTube videos of the CEO, and sold myself on the idea. None of my four old printers at the house were hooked up properly. I pulled out some notebook paper and a pencil because my old office pens were out of ink. It must have been Ben's pencil because it was written in purple and smelled like grapes. It reminded me of the scratch-and-sniff stickers I loved as a kid. It was my new favorite writing utensil. I stared at the blank sheet and my categories for health, personal, and work goals for 1, 5, 10, and 15 years. I had nothing. The traumas had sucked the *"joie de vivre"* out of me. I'd been living in a detached, aimless purgatory, especially since the accident. I had told myself I was giving myself space and time to heal, but really, I was floating along, going nowhere. If I wanted to work my way up to store manager at Lululemon and make $150,000 a year, I had to come up with something. Out of nowhere, I just started making things up. Get a tattoo within a year. It was something that I'd always wanted but was never brave enough or sure of what to get. Learn how to surf. Visit five new countries. Reconcile with my parents (put that one on the fifteen-year track). Write a book. Read one hundred books.

Work at Lululemon within a year, and then be a store manager within five years. Have the ability to retire, independently wealthy, by forty-five. I kept writing until all areas were filled in. The next day, I went to the mailbox store in Sumner and printed some worksheets. I wrote "see attached" in the blanks and drove around with my resume and goals in the car until the next time I went by the store so I could give him a copy when I applied. But my goal was to start working there within a year, and I didn't feel rushed to apply. Eventually, my crisp copies got a bit smashed in my bag, and I still haven't applied. But, as the year went on, things started happening.

Opportunities popped up everywhere to put me on track for my newly made-up goals. I had taken up the habit of watching Super Soul Sunday on OWN, and one weekend saw Oprah interview a few young people as part of a panel. One of them was Mastin Kipp, whose Facebook profile and blog were called *"The Daily Love."* His insights resonated with me, and with one click, I was following him on Facebook. Not long after following him, he announced a twenty-eight-day writer's retreat in Bali, where you could *"become your hero."* Write the entire first draft of your book or screenplay in one month. He had done it once before by himself and was inviting a group of thirteen people to do it with him, with writing coaches and outings around Bali.

I was intrigued. There are all kinds of tours and cruises, but this was an opportunity I knew I couldn't create for myself and one that might not ever happen again. I did the application online on my phone and got an email request to set up a phone interview with Mastin's assistant. I scheduled the time for a few weeks out and decided I would see how that went first before I decided to commit fully. In the meantime, I began talking to a self-publisher about publishing. I had tried writing my story twice in the past two years, once while couchbound. I knew it would happen, just not how, but I also knew they were one way to get it done sooner rather than later. It turned out I could also get it done sooner by writing the entire first draft in one month. My talk with the assistant left me with nothing but a warm, fuzzy feeling that positively reinforced my intuition to go for it. I then decided I would go if I were invited and if it cost less than my conceivable max. It did, $1 less. So I signed up and hoped no other life disaster would stop me from getting to Bali because I had been through enough.

The Bali trip was killing two birds with one stone because I also wanted to visit new countries, and Indonesia was a new one for me. So was Greece, and my girlfriend Sage was getting married the third week of September in Milos, a small island in Greece. All my Australian friends were going. It was going to be awesome, and I was going to be ready to travel again. I hadn't been overseas since Florence in January 2010, and I was longing to get away. I was grateful my settlement would allow me the option not to work and continue healing while also getting to travel to these events. Since the Bali retreat came after the wedding, I decided to extend my trip to allow me to go back to Italy, and even to visit other exchange student friends before the wedding. I decided to leave on September 1, the day after Teddy's seventh birthday.

Chapter 26

ANNULMENT

They say you can't change the past. But I've learned there are a couple of ways we do it anyway. One way in law, the other in church law. In law, you can make a motion for an order called "*Nunc pro tunc.*" It's an order the court can sign on that day as if it were signed however many years ago. It's a way of redoing today what was incorrectly done before. Like an acquittal after a criminal conviction, an incorrect civil order can be fixed. It's the court's way of correcting mistakes. I've had to apply for that kind of order before to fix a child support order with incorrect numbers. The church way is an annulment. Meaning had I stayed happily married, our sacramental marriage would have been valid. But an inquiry into everything leading up to and including our wedding day could lead the church to conclude our marriage was, in fact, invalid, and an annulment could be granted as if it never really happened. This was the way I could reach back to the old me, the fiercely Catholic me that was raised so strictly, and give her a gift. Make her feel better. She is still a part of me, of course, but I no longer feel bound to practice my faith in the context of Catholicism. I feel like it's bigger than that and like there are as many ways toward God as there are people. Still, after the civil divorce decree was entered in January, I felt like something was still there. Something else to undo, untie. I applied for an annulment. I also googled how to leave the Catholic church formally. But that would make more sense after my annulment was granted, and it takes two years.

It costs $500 to file, and an advocate submits and responds to paperwork on my behalf. I called St. Andrew's to find out who the advocate(s) might be. It turned out one was a former client of mine. She gladly agreed for my annulment to be her last. I was grateful. In over twenty years, she only had one not go through. I emailed JD, shared my feeling that I still felt kind of married, and told him I would apply. He said he felt we hadn't been married since our last fight in April 2011. Perfect. I let him know to ignore the paperwork so that it would go through more easily. That way, if either of us met Catholics in the future we wanted to marry, we'd also be free to do so. He didn't care, of course.

There were over seven pages of questions, each with four or five subparts. I wasn't going to let myself be the reason for any delay, and it took me three days to get through all the questions. There was a lot about our upbringings, and I slowly realized how much that had affected and interfered with our ability to sustain a lifelong relationship. Especially his mother having left when he was so young. Especially my parents never showed us how conflicts are resolved; all those conversations were hidden behind the closed doors of Dad's den. I submitted my thirty-five pages of testimony. I listed Jennah, my aunt, and my parents as witnesses. I knew my parents would be motivated to say anything that might help an annulment be granted to *"save my soul."* And they all were the type to return that kind of paperwork promptly. Away it went. I eventually got a response letter that indicated there were two canon laws under which they might grant the petition. One applied for me, another for him. The old me smiled.

Chapter 27

NEW NOSE

Besides an annulment and the upcoming travel, I started to do a little fantasy shopping. I knew I couldn't live on my settlement forever. I didn't have to work yet, and there was something I'd always wanted to change. My nose. Ever since high school, I wanted it just a bit smaller. It would look awkward for me to have a drastic facial alteration, but I never cared for its size or the slight bump from the side. And I knew that, as you age, your ears and nose keep growing. I mostly wanted to look like I felt I did—until I saw myself in the mirror or a photo, and the tinge of desire for a slightly smaller nose would frequently arise. I was no stranger to cosmetic improvements, having had substantial work done to straighten and whiten my teeth and having undergone a breast reduction the summer before my year in Italy. I drank and ate so much in Australia that I came home with a huge stomach, chest, and multiple chins. I became a rower my freshman year and lost all the weight and chins but not the chest.

Insurance covered the reduction because over three-and-a-half pounds was removed, leaving me then a C cup. It was painful, 300 stitches in each one, but so worth it. I carried my backpack all over Europe instead of my chest. So, my appearance was already drastically different from what it would have been without dental and chest work… a nose job was something I didn't expect I'd ever regret, having wanted it for so long. I secretly looked up a Bellevue surgeon, Dr. Neil, and booked an appointment. I was so excited. I figured if he told me that my nose was fine as it was, I would listen. I told Ben because I couldn't keep my secret. He said I didn't need it, and I agreed, but it was something I had always wanted. I went to my appointment, describing my wishes for a smaller overall nose and the hump being gone. Dr. Neil said he could also raise the droopy tip. I had a droopy tip! I didn't even know that. I had seen his work, and he achieved a natural effect. His assistant had me set a date for May 7 so that most of my swelling would be gone in time for the wedding in Greece.

May 7 came and went, and the surgery was done in-office, nothing like the trauma of the metal repair to my leg. It was as painful as getting your wisdom teeth removed. It was swollen at first. Ridiculously swollen. Luckily, I was hardly bruised. I took it easy; healing was my thing. My roommate and Ben knew and a few friends, but not everyone, and no family. I missed our monthly sibling dinner, and I missed hot yoga for a month, waiting for the swelling to go down enough so I could breathe easily through a whole class. When I started getting out again, most people didn't even notice, but I knew, and I felt good. I felt like I looked more like me as if that's why God made plastic surgeons, so we can look the way we feel.

Chapter 28

MILKSHAKE DATES WITH PAPA

With my nose fairly healed and my leg bothering me less on long drives, I decided it was time to start visiting my grandpa. Papa was moved into a nursing home after Grandma died, and I still hadn't seen him since before the time I did at Harborview. He still loves his milkshakes, so I decided I would bring him one. I packed Teddy and myself into my new black BMW 318ti with its 'VOLTURI" license plates, and we drove over the mountains to Wenatchee. I didn't want to cross paths with my parents, so we went on a Sunday, stayed the night in a hotel, and visited Papa Monday morning. Both Mom and Dad would be at work. Papa is closing in on ninety years old, and mostly old age was not kind to him. He's suffered strokes, and his hands don't really work anymore except to claw things. He can't walk or move himself around much at all. They don't put his teeth in, glasses on, or hearing aids in for him. But he can hold a milkshake. He was sitting in his wheelchair at one of the dining tables in a smelly, carpeted dining area while 1950s music played in the background. His eyes lit up when he saw me. He smiled a big, toothless smile. I almost cried but instead found my voice and cheerily greeted him with, *"Hi, Papa!"* I got him situated with his shake while Teddy greeted Papa's co-residents. Papa didn't talk, but it didn't matter. I wanted to spill my traumas out to him, but what could he say or do? And I was there for him, not for me. I held his arm and then his hand as he drank and fell asleep. He'd wake up about once every twenty minutes or so and drink a bit more, smile at me, and fall asleep again as I held him. It took about three hours for him to finish the shake, and I stayed with him, letting Teddy say goodbye as I kissed his forehead before we headed out. I found out Papa didn't get visited often—mostly only on Sundays by my parents and now and then by my siblings—so I decided to go every other week, or every week when I could, until my big trip. On our second visit, Papa smiled and asked, *"Who's that?"* as he pointed at Teddy. He repeated Teddy's name after me and smiled. Our milkshake dates continued all summer. I would be away for two months traveling but would see him again in November. I was amazed how he would hang in there with so little he could do for himself, and I hope he felt less alone and a little more loved from our visits.

Whenever I missed Grandma, I would find food we used to eat at her house, like Golden Graham's cereal. She loved birds, so any birdsong reminds me of her. I plant my flower boxes now with the ones that she used to have at her house when she taught me to pick away the dead buds to allow the new ones to bloom. I like to think the shooting stars I see are her waving from heaven. Once, I was feeling sad for no apparent reason and got myself a Happy Meal like how Grandma and Papa used to take us out for a treat. I texted my brother later to ask him about the date. He confirmed it was the year anniversary of Grandma's passing.

I noticed Grandma and Papa's wedding picture was missing in Papa's room at the nursing home. I found out from my sister that my mom had the original. I preferred to avoid communicating with her, but I felt the one photo Papa saw above his dresser daily for over sixty years deserved to be in the room where he would spend his final days. He lived with strangers, and Alzheimer's left him with less recent memories than distant ones. On my last visit before my big trip, I checked, and a copy of the wedding photo was there as it always had been. It felt more like Papa's room than before, and I gave him his milkshake.

Chapter 29

E-BATTLE WITH MOM AND DAD

A few family events came up in July. My nephew John's second birthday, my niece Marie's baptism, and my other nephew Joseph's first birthday. I had been attending the monthly sibling dinners for about nine months, and I had agreed to attend these celebrations, where my parents were sure to be. In anticipation of this being difficult for me, I went back to my therapist, Kari, for the summer. I wanted to prepare for dealing with my parents and also to work my issues with them for myself since I didn't feel comfortable openly discussing things. I hated how they looked at me through a kind of bipolar, or unstable, filter. I hated what they helped do to me, and I knew they would do it again. I hated how it felt like they would always look at me differently, worse, not better, than before. It seemed they believed that if it hadn't been for JD's cheating and that trauma, I wouldn't be bipolar and would be living my normal life. Ironically, I was and have been living more as myself than ever. However, they never got to see the real me before. Instead, I kept giving them the façade-me and they kept treating me as a child. I was first myself in Australia. Then a bit more in Italy. Now, free of the marriage, the law practice, Catholicism, and them, I've been rediscovering what I love and just being myself. The free me looked alien to them; they tortured the old me, and I had to make peace with my decision to let them go.

Ironically, they made it easy for me. I didn't talk to them hardly at all at the first birthday pool party. Ben went with me. With him there, I didn't feel the need to drink or get high to be around them. I also had some support from my sisters-in-law, who had reached out to me through my aunt. They were the compassionate and nonjudgmental types that I wished my parents could be. They cheerily greeted Ben and I, and we spoke more with them than anyone else. Also, all the sibling dinners kind of paid off because I sensed a shift. The family was no longer us kids and Mom and Dad; it was us siblings and their spouses and kids. It wasn't too bad, but Dad was just as standoffish as Mom. He later emailed an apology:

Good to see you and Ben. Sorry, I was such a pill; my doctor put me on some new meds that made me feel sicker than a dog. Love, Dad

I didn't hold back in my response:

Thanks for apologizing; I'm not sure I've ever heard you apologize, Dad. Although you didn't say hello, you did try twice talking with me, while Mom didn't try once. I can understand how meds can affect behavior, hope you get it worked out and feel better soon.

The distance between us, though, doesn't have to do with your behavior at a BBQ. I felt hurt and betrayed by you and Mom more than by JD in the last few years. Because of many things both of you have said and done, I don't trust you and don't want you in my life or know details about my life. I assume you currently believe that I had an alleged dormant bipolar diagnosis and that the trauma of the cheating means I'm now full-blown bipolar for life? If that is the case, I don't know if I will ever be able to have a relationship with you. Even if I were bipolar, you should know that your comment that bipolar people destroy families and you won't let me destroy yours makes me not keen to have a relationship.

I asked for the Valium prescription to take at Jason's wedding to keep it together, be there for Jason, and not have you find out what was going on with JD and me. I needed the ability to work through the possibility of reconciling with him without your interference or judgment. But I needed support and had no one I trusted and no coping skills to deal with such hurt except for medicating, which my doctor obliged without concern for me being home alone and no one to monitor side effects for me. When the stress prevented me from sleeping, my doctor prescribed Ambien CR, then Celexa, lorazepam, and more Valium, before the hospital gave me about six more prescriptions... but the details or other professional opinions I've obtained since don't matter if you're 100% vested in your belief. I'm not sure when I might be ready to continue communicating or to attempt a reconciliation, especially without an apology or the willingness to consider I may not be bipolar.

The indescribable trauma of the hospitalizations still affects me. Until I recover from that, I will likely continue to intentionally keep my distance but attend the kids' events to preserve my relationships with Jason and Lily. I initially continued to see you so you could see I was "ok" to prevent you from trying to do anything else. I appreciate you continuing to leave me alone for a while, but if I'm mistaken about any assumptions, please let me know.

A few more exchanges later, I finally just asked for an apology, giving him an opening, letting him know what I needed to feel respected and to keep them in my life. He refused. She didn't apologize, either. He basically summed up that he did the best he could to help. He explained he's not perfect and will continue to love me unconditionally with all his flaws. I decided to let go. That wasn't good enough. I don't want their kind of love anymore. The kind where there's right and wrong and no apologies when your best efforts really hurt the other person. I told both him and my mom that I was done. I attended the other two events alone. The baptism was a bit strange, but at least my sisters-in-law were still in town. I sat in the back of the church and watched all of them smile in the front row. I didn't even remember all the parts of the mass anymore, and some of the words had changed. I finally bailed when it was time for communion and took a few minutes for myself downstairs in the restroom. I got a text from my sister's father-in-law, who had passed by my corner after communion. I let him know I was okay and would be back up when it was over. It felt like *Sesame Street*, and I was the thing that was not like the others. It was a little lonely, but I was okay with it at the same time. I could visit their world, my old world, but continue to live in mine.

Chapter 30

MY FIRST TATTOO

Thanks to Thomas at Lululemon, I had goals to accomplish. In my world of meditation and yoga, it seemed like everyone had tattoos, and I'd always wanted one. It took me forever to decide what to get, but having survived so much *"life mud,"* I decided on a small black outline of a lotus. Ben was always down to get a new tattoo, and he wanted a couple of birds on a wire on his right wrist. On his left wrist was his blank *"to-do"* list, which I got for him one snow day before my accident. I chickened out that day. I still didn't know what I wanted or where, and the guys in that shop were a little scary. With the little lotus picture on my phone, Ben and I went to the tattoo shop my roommate Angel told us about to make our appointment.

I made a quick stop in the restroom and then followed the sound of voices to the back room, where I found Ben. Angel had told me to ask for James, so when I saw who Ben was talking to, I asked, *"You're not James, are you?"* and he peered up at me over his black-rimmed glasses. Instantly, I felt something. It totally caught me off guard because I hadn't felt something like it before. I wanted James. He was nearing fifty and bald, yet nothing about him turned me off. I wanted to be around his energy and sleep with him, too, at least once. It had to be. I snapped out of it and casually made our appointment for the next day. As we got outside and walked back to my car, Ben said, *"Really?!!"* I giggled. *"You noticed?"* He said yeah, and he confirmed that he also noticed it was mutual. When we got home, I told Angel, *"I want James." "NOOOoooo way! I will kick your ass!"* she fumed. She reminded me that James was in a motorcycle club and knew from experience how bad things could get for me if I upset him or if it ended badly. I really didn't get that feeling, and instead of promising it wouldn't happen, I agreed to think it over.

I'd been having some fun since I ended things with Ben almost two years prior, trying some online dating and some friends with benefits. I had also just taken about four months off, guys altogether. I wanted some time and space for myself to reflect on what I really wanted in that area of my life. I decided I wanted to really like whoever I was with. And I really liked James.

When we went back to get our tattoos the next day, Ben and I sat in the waiting area while James ate his late lunch. He was as lax about time as I was, but as I sat, I thought about running. *"I haven't run away yet,"* I said. He gave me a sly smile and said, *"I have a guy outside the door."* It sounded half ominous, half joke. Rather than test it out, I went first. I showed James my design. He smirked. "Hold on." He came back with an outline of a much prettier and much larger lotus.

"Yours is okay, but this will make you want more tattoos." I loved it, and it was drawn by him, for me. It hurt, some needles more than others. But James touching my arm felt good. I trusted him, and I let him hurt me as his art was inked into my arm. I just kept breathing. He went slowly, taking breaks each time I thought I couldn't take it anymore. Ben squirmed, having to wait so long for his turn. He did, though, make sure to let James know that I was single and that he thought James and I should go out. That led to some fun texting while Ben got his birds. As James finished up

in black ink, he said he could add some color. He remarked that I seemed like a colorful person—at the time, I did have a purple streak in my blonde hair that I let my girlfriend Amy keep putting back in because it reminded me of Florence. I didn't want it to end, and we agreed that he put in light purple shading. My lotus was complete. Instead of admiring the ring that used to sparkle on my left hand, I would start driving around admiring the lotus on the inside of my left wrist. Beautiful things like that grow from mud, and I felt I had grown from my life mud. I am the girl with the lotus tattoo. I was so excited to go to my next yoga class and to go out with James.

James and I texted off and on, but I didn't confess to Angel that I ended up going out with and hooking up with him one night until after it happened. She was right. I googled him before we went out, and he had quite the history, enough to give my dad a stroke. I was even more down.

He texted me spur of the moment, and we had a fun dinner followed by more fun at his place. It had to happen, and I was happy it did. We keep in touch. I have more canvas, and he has more ink.

Chapter 31

THE BAR COMPLAINT

With a successful annulment underway, I felt like I was on a roll. I could also finally get up the nerve to complain about the past actions of my attorney. For me, a lawsuit didn't feel right. Instead, I felt a bar complaint was the way to go. It could affect his license, but I hoped it would at least affect his behavior. A complaint was easy to submit. I could do it all online. I had to put down the case number of the involuntary commitment. I sucked it up and went to the court in person because those records could only be accessed by me, in person, and with my ID. They were sealed. The clerk couldn't find anything. I knew I hadn't imagined it, so I had her search my name all different ways. Nothing. It should have shown up as Case Type 6 under my name with a simple public Washington courts online search. All that came up were a couple of traffic tickets and my divorce proceedings. I breathed a sigh of relief. It meant someone looking into me would have to look really, really hard to see it had even happened.

I still needed to access the records, though, so I made sure that stirring the pot to get access wouldn't lead to the online system being updated. They said no, that would only happen by my request. I went home to dig through my records for the case number and found it on one of the releases for information I'd signed to allow my attorney to access my medical records. My online complaint was complete. I pressed submit. I got an email acknowledging receipt. I felt relieved. I had finally stood up for myself and was again reaching back into the past to help my old self feel better.

It backfired. A couple of weeks later, I got two letters in the mail from the Washington State Bar Association disciplinary office, one thicker than the other. I opened the thinner one first. It notified me that what my attorney had done by proceeding with the hearing over my objection to the judge knowing my father and not requiring her to recuse herself was a legitimate "judgment call" and not, in any way they could figure, an ethical violation. They were dismissing the complaint against my attorney. I assumed the second envelope would contain the means to appeal their decision. No. Instead, it was putting me on notice that the WSBA had initiated its complaint against me, questioning my capacity to practice law because the contents of my original complaint indicated that I had been involuntarily committed. My stomach dropped, along with my jaw. What the fuck?

I was so upset. I read the rules. I knew I was fine, but what would it take to prove it? They could take my deposition and subpoena ALL my medical records at MY expense. I was scared. I cried. At first, I didn't want anyone to know. Then I remembered how well that worked for me with JD's cheating, and I reached out to my new inner circle. I told Ben first. Then I called my aunt, and later Sophie. Did I want to relive the trauma to save a license I wasn't even using? Or would I give up and resign in lieu of undergoing the torture of such an extensive investigation?

I surrendered. I decided to trust that, whatever happened, I would accept and make decisions along the way as the process progressed. It weighed on me. Heavily. I got Kari's help because

I'd been using her to deal with the unresolved issues with Mom and Dad all summer. Since I felt unable to get through to them, I resolved it for myself by working with her and accepting what was instead of longing for something that might never be. Kari made a report that I submitted with my response to the complaint. I had little time before my planned travels, which were coming up in less than a month. Luckily, Kari's report helped with my annulment, too. I still remember how her words both soothed and validated how I'd felt while my marriage unraveled:

"Husband wasn't willing to be sexually faithful and did not compassionately support wife during her temporary disability."

A bar representative had to meet with me, and they wanted it to happen before I left. I agreed to meet at the Sumner library because I didn't want to be judged for my house not being perfectly clean. I remembered how JD used to white-glove inspect everything whenever he came home from work. *"My TV is dusty!"* he would growl. He would always find something to complain about, even after I hired a housekeeper. I gave up and let him find something so that he'd stop looking. I wasn't up for a *"bar inspection,"* too.

We met at the library, and I asked what the purpose of the meeting was. *"It's a formality,"* she explained. I breathed a sigh of relief. Apparently, there have been times they found attorneys who were in the middle of a batshit crazy phase, throwing their files into the street and wandering around outside their house. I told her I'd never heard of anything like that occurring. She said it was their job to keep things like that under wraps and initiate a special disability proceeding and status. I summed up my story, and she took notes. I kept to the facts, filtering and not letting myself get into the things that could still bring me to tears. I made sure my parents would not be contacted. She assured me they would not and that she expected my case to be dismissed, especially upon their receipt of an evaluation from my therapist that said I was fully capable of practicing law again if I chose to do so. I was relieved but fearful they might also require my court documents. I offered to get them in November if they were necessary, and asked for an email instead of a letter upon the dismissal. Still not sure I would rather resign than undergo a full inquiry, I let it go and waited.

They knew that I would be out of the country for two months, and I would get an email if it were resolved before my return.

Chapter 32

TWO GOODBYES

In December, when our divorce papers were finalized, JD asked his attorney to put in the paperwork that he would give me his car on April 2, what would have been our wedding anniversary. We hardly spoke. I'd been so hurt; I had no interest in staying friends. I told him that all we had was a shared history and that any further relationship would not happen. When April 2 came around, he asked for more time. The car he was trying to purchase fell through for some reason. This happened again, and then in June, he asked if he could just keep it. He said that he was flying as a copilot because the company wasn't doing well. He was making less money and wanted me to let him just keep the car.

I reeled at the email. And I knew he was paying $1,500 a month for ten days a month at home at his condo in West Seattle. He could make some changes and survive. I felt that by negotiating for the car, I had earned it, and I wasn't ready to go back to work. I told him I would sell it to him, or he would have to give it back. He didn't respond. So, I put a call in to his attorney's office. That did the trick. He said he'd be back in July and would let me know then. I think he wanted to be done with me, not owe me monthly car payments, and he decided to give the car back. He brought it to the house.

I heard the doorbell and put Teddy on his leash. We walked outside. I figured I'd get the keys and take Teddy for a walk to process and calm down. He looked up and saw Teddy. *"Do me a favor; put the dog back in the house,"* he barked, while the accent I knew so well lingered in the air. He couldn't handle seeing Teddy. If it would have helped him or if he had asked, I would have even allowed him visitation, but he wanted nothing to do with us. I let Teddy wait inside. I looked at JD. He was wearing his sunglasses, so I couldn't even see his eyes. I don't know why he wouldn't show his face. He filmed a walk-around of the car, pausing a few seconds with his iPhone camera on me before he shut it off. I assume his lawyer told him a video would prevent me from arguing there was any damage. I hadn't pulled anything like that all along, so I don't know why he feared it now. Still, he stormed over to me and let go of the key and fob without touching my hand. He said he left some of my Australian pictures in the trunk for me. I asked for the second set of keys, but he didn't have them. And he left. No hug, no eye contact even. I said bye, and he stomped off, getting into his friend's car.

I stood there for a minute. It was sad. He seemed as mad as the night he threatened to kill me. He seemed like he might never learn how to be happy. I pray he does because no one and nothing else can make him happy. I peeked into the trunk. It was a box of our wedding photos that he'd cleared out when he left, maybe not to upset the formerly unstable me. It felt like I was looking at someone else's life. The bride in the photos would never have predicted this moment. I brought the box inside and took Teddy on our river loop walk.

Ben was struggling to find a job around town, and his car needed repairs. He was trying to find something within walking distance. I was willing to let him continue earning his keep around the house, but not extras like car repairs, gas, etc. Trying to work out other options, he had been in contact with an ex-girlfriend and her mom on the East Coast. They would let him stay for free and had a few jobs lined up for him. They even bought his plane ticket. He knew I would be gone for a couple of months and felt like it was time for him to start getting ahead on his own. He was nervous about leaving, but I encouraged him and let him know that he could come back anytime. If I were going to let the house go, I would give him a heads-up so he could get the rest of his things.

He was fidgety as I drove him to the airport. I let him smoke a cigarette, blowing his smoke out the window. He was nervous to fly. He got teary. I tried not to. I calmly reassured him, and he felt better. It was time for him to fly out of my home, that had become a safe nest for him. It was time for me to fly away, too. We saved and cared for each other for two years. We would miss his August 14 birthday (same as my sister's) together, but his tattoo was his advance present. I had done that airport drive dozens of times every year with JD. It was strange to say goodbye to Ben the way I'd so often let JD go. We parked, and I went inside with him to make sure he at least found his way to security. He stayed upbeat, and we hugged. I kept it together until I reached the parking garage. I paid for my parking while tears rolled down my cheeks. I missed him already.

Chapter 33

TWO MONTHS OVERSEAS

It was early. I was driving to my BMW repair shop to get my car an oil check and a once-over before I took my last trip over the mountains to see Papa. The air was crisp, and the sky was ice blue. Because of the traffic, I ended up driving east on Highway 18 to go north to Bellevue. The sky held my attention. It was like a sky that should soar above an arctic tundra. A sky I'd never seen before. I'm always amazed at how the sky can be more beautiful than a Michelangelo painting. The other night, driving home from getting my hair done, it was shimmering gold and pink and sparkly, too, like the clouds were lit from the inside and dusted with glitter. When did I stop looking at the sky? How can it change so frequently, look ominous one moment then amazing and full of promise? The rainbow, I was taught, was a symbol of God promising he wouldn't do that to you again. Hah. Promises meant nothing to me now.

I discovered, after everything, that all I really need is to breathe. Everything I'll ever need will always be available inside me. I have heard so many times what doesn't kill you makes you stronger. But to me, it's simpler: What doesn't kill you, didn't kill you. So now what? Whatever I want. Me. Not you. The world can have its expectations, and every *"should."* The word *"should"* no longer exists in my world. That word got me to ground zero. All that really matters is now because that is all I have. I can still get weepy thinking about the past. Focusing on the unknowable future causes me anxiety. So, I stick to where I am. Here. Now. Breathing. Free. Taking life in with all my senses. Refocusing. Dreaming. Being a steward of this body, this life, this world. Being. No longer doing. I no longer identify with doing; I'm not what I do. I'm just me. I'm not my name. I'm not what's happened to me. I'm not my pain. I am free, love, now, abundance, peace, light…

I was meditating before yoga the other day, and while doing some *"I am"* phrases, a couple of words came to me impromptu:

I am…*ancient*.

I am…*heroic.*

It turned out I was my own hero. It took faith in myself, faith in my gut, faith in there being something on the other side of my version of hell. After losing everything that used to mean everything to me, all I had left was all that really mattered. Breath. Peace. Love. Teddy. Kitten. Unconditional love is better demonstrated by animals than by humans. It's so ironic. We're the "intelligent species." But we're emotionally unevolved. I'm discovering what I love, who I am, and what resonates with me. Fitness. Yoga. Meditating. Writing. Photography. Travel. Friends. Some family. Resilience. Freedom. Permission to grieve. Trusting my gut. My gut, my intuition, and the feedback I get from emotions and my body are no longer white noise in the background of a stressful, busy life. Quiet doesn't scare me. Simple things are wonderful and priceless. Letting go and creating space in my life for things and people that really support and fulfill me is a new skill.

I was getting ready to leave for two whole months, first reconnecting with old friends, then off to Bali. I wanted to meet one more guy before I went. Ian was a decade my junior, but we already seemed to connect via messaging. He cracked me up, and we hadn't even met. He had just broken his leg, too, playing soccer. I first saw him through the latest popular app for dating, and we had a mutual Facebook friend, one of my tanning salon girls. We'd been chatting for a month because I thought he'd be as laid up as I was with my leg. I figured out he was getting around much better, much faster, so we met up at an Irish bar near his place in Redmond. He gave me a one-legged standing hug and a huge smile when I found him. His blue eyes sparkled with life while we chatted away. He was fun and happy. The happiest guy I had ever met. He smiled as much as I did. I wanted to be around him more and agreed to go back to his place. He warned me his dog Chloe would bark at me at first, then calm down. We walked into the kitchen and Chloe, part pit, bounded downstairs to greet him, then me. He came over and gave me a sniff, letting me pat him hello without a bark or growl as if he already knew me. Ian was shocked. We ended up dog-piled in his bed for the night.

He cooked scrambled eggs and sliced some fruit for us. We hung out a bit and took forever saying goodbye in his car, but he ended up also giving me an airport ride. He'd brought a goodie bag of magazines and word search puzzles, my favorite. I gave him one of my new favorite lip balms, flavored with milk and honey, that he'd liked when we met... and I know we'll hang out when I get back. We tossed around the idea of going to the World Cup in Brazil the next year...either way, I was happy to like someone again.

Chapter 34

SWEDEN AND FRANCE

I was on the plane, finally putting distance between myself and so many places I felt trapped. I was free and on my way. A few hours into the flight, I had to stretch my legs and make my way to the tiny airplane bathroom. I caught a look at myself in the mirror. The spark was back. I couldn't miss it, even in the warped bathroom mirror of the Airbus 330, taking me and a bunch of other people to Amsterdam. I saw it. And it wasn't just because of Ian (okay, maybe a little). But really, it was because I am back. Not just back—better. Than ever. As long as what doesn't kill me still doesn't kill me.

In Stockholm, everyone looked like me. Tall, blonde, and blue-eyed. It was fun to so easily blend in until I opened my mouth to speak English instead of Swedish. I had an incredible time catching up with my girlfriend Hanna, who I hadn't seen in person since we were in Australia together almost twenty years prior. With that shared year in common, we launched into the next phase of what I know will be a lifelong friendship. She last knew me when I was free and 10,000 miles away from home, and when we reconnected, I was back to being away from home and free. In just one afternoon at the botanical garden, we quickly and easily shared two decades of stories, and although it was hard to leave, I knew that I would not let another twenty years pass before we hung out again. The same happened with my girlfriend Inga, living in Malmo. She has beautiful twin girls that were just over a year old. We fell right back into our friendship as she juggled the twins. We even snuck in an afternoon at a two-hundred-year-old sauna on the sea.

I headed down to France next to see Celine. Our hearts burst when we first saw each other again at the Biarritz airport. Her eyes welled up, and I couldn't hold back my tears either. She had her youngest girl in her arms, and we smooshed her between us in a teary bear hug. I stayed a week with Celine and her husband, and three kids. It was like I was their exchange student. We, too, fell right back into our prior connection. I rediscovered how much love was waiting for me in the friends I had around the world, and I was so grateful to find it everywhere I went.

Celine's husband also helped me toward another of my goals. He took me surfing for a day. He took me out in the water and launched me onto the waves by pushing me when the right one came. When I finished screaming, I remembered to try and get up, first on my knees and then a few times on my feet. At first, I could stand for only a few seconds before the board flipped out from under me. He said I was standing too far back. He must have launched me over twenty times. I was going hoarse from screaming, and I might have lost a contact lens because I could hardly see out one eye. He laughed and asked me if I was a pirate or a surfer. Surfer all the way. I kept saying *"one more time"* until my leg couldn't take it anymore.

I almost missed my flight when it was time to go, but knowing I was welcome to come back, maybe even for a whole summer, kept me from crying as I made my way to my gate.

Chapter 35

ITALY

I had a layover in Paris on my way to Florence. I used it as a chance to recharge by staying overnight on a yacht on the Seine River. I had to do the dinner cruise and arrived at the dock with time to settle into my room and take a few pictures from the top deck. Sitting at my table, it was as I anticipated. I was the only single table on the boat. There were mostly couples, one set of girlfriends, and one foursome. The couples reminded me of what I once had and will have again when I'm ready. The girlfriends reminded me of what I will always have. But what I had that night was a date with Paris. I ordered champagne, then a half bottle of Bordeaux. It was beautiful, the dinner and the cruise. We passed Notre Dame before a few loops around the Eiffel Tower. I loved seeing all the bridges from the water. On my honeymoon we visited Paris but stayed on land. It was a memorable night that I enjoyed all for myself.

I realized, arriving at Charles-de-Gaulle the next morning, that my flight to Florence included a layover in Austria. That must have been why it was only $100. So, leaving Vienna, I chatted with the woman who ended up sitting next to me. She was friendly and looked like an Austrian version of myself, right down to her puffy vest, just like my favorite red one that I left at home. I shared what I was up to and the briefest possible version of my story. Then Austrian me said, *"Maybe the universe has something planned for you."* She also remarked how wonderful it was to travel because meeting people away from home creates a connection that never goes away. I was wholly in agreement, as I'd been experiencing it through Sweden and France. And then, after we both shared that we don't have children, she said a phrase that used to irritate me: *"Everything happens for a reason."* For the first time, I didn't mind hearing it.

Walking out of the airport in Florence, it smelled like home. Every smell brought me back to my junior year and all the other visits since. I got four days to get my fill before heading off to Greece for Sage's wedding. I was staying at the pensione that I lived in before, shared bathrooms and all. It was cheap, and that made me feel less guilty about doing a little shopping. I had my leather trench coat with me, as I needed to have it remade to fit the slimmer me. Thanks to the swimming, hot yoga, and my trainer, I was down sixty pounds, below even my pre-accident weight. I was uncomfortably heavy after spending four months couchbound, but I slowly and successfully worked it off once I was mobile. I went into Renzo's leather store, and he welcomed me back with wine. I left my trench to be remade but also left with a new, shorter, and fitted coat that really complemented my skin, hair, and eyes. It was a celebration coat. And no one was there to tell me no.

I went to my shoe store, Antica Cuoio, and picked up one more pair of boots. I was running out of room in my luggage, so for a second pair, I went to their outlet store for ballet flats. At the outlet, I met Gemella. She sold me shoes and some philosophy, as she had been a psychology major. Like a fairy godmother, she pranced around the store, bringing me different sizes and colors to try while showering me with encouragement. The ones with patent leather woven with regular leather were the cutest to me, with patent toes to match. I momentarily looked at a brown and black pair before she stopped me, saying, *"You don't need any more sad things."* She guided me back to the light and dark pink ones with cream patent toes. She spoke in Italian to me, and her messages were as beautiful as her words. Life is about endings and beginnings. Each new beginning is better than the last because we've learned and grown from our mistakes. She might as well have waved a magic wand over me as she said my next love would be even more amazing than the last because of how I'd changed… but I needed to love myself first. I can love myself better than anyone else can, and when I'm happy with myself, I can be happy with anyone else. *"La vita e' bella, Tesoro,"* she said, then asked me to make her dream by sending her postcards from my travels.

Chapter 36

A WEDDING IN GREECE

A plane, taxi, and eight-hour ferry boat ride later, I was in Milos. Milos was like a hug for my soul. The sun was warm. The salty air greeted me each day, and the cool water would become warm after a brief swim. The breeze gently dried me so that I didn't even need the beach towel that I picked up at the Pollonia *"general store."* I had expected a beach scene from what I saw while it was folded and wrapped in plastic. I got to my room to open it and found a huge donkey with blankets piled on his back and *"GREECE DONKEY"* written in big red capital letters across the bottom. I had to keep it now. The quiet on the island was calming, and the waves gently lapping at the shore outside my studio balcony gently woke me and invited me for a daily morning swim.

Hanging out the week leading up to the wedding, I got to catch up with many of my Aussie friends, including Sage's and Rina's parents. Each of the girls, Holly, Rina, Alina, and Sage, asked me what had happened. I gave each of them different, short versions, keeping myself above tears. After they were all up to speed, Alina asked me, *"So what makes you happy now?"*

"To breathe," I said simply.

"What?"

She seemed to want more.

"To breathe. I can meditate like a motherfucker."

I shared my story with Sage's parents, who I had been close to also when I lived in Australia. They both apologized for what had happened and how I had no support. They were and would always be on Team Sarah and offered that I could come to them anytime I ever needed to be sad. Sage's dad took me for a spin on the dance floor at her wedding. He shared that he admired my courage and that he couldn't have survived what I went through. I cried and took in his fatherly love as we danced. He gave me the moment I had been longing for with my father.

Sage's dad also introduced me to his nephew, Marco, who he called the *"Don Juan"* of Malta. I chatted with him, and we discovered that we both were cheated on in our marriages. We had accidental traumatic physical injuries in common as well. We had so much common ground it was easy to feel a growing mutual bond. We kept talking alongside the dance floor. He was just taller than me, with dark olive skin, gray-dappled dark hair, and a slightly scruffy face. His dreamy, soft brown eyes penetrated my blue gaze. We held long periods of eye contact and touch, our hands resting next to each other on the balcony rail or our shoulders gently leaning into one another. We sat next to each other on the 3 a.m. bus ride back to our studios. He walked me to mine, and we parted ways. I got a Facebook message from him as soon as I got back to my room:

Found you!!!

Did you say room 8?

Adds to a series of coincidences.

Yes, I'm in room 8... are you as well??

Yes!!!

Crazy or what

That's almost too much!! Wow

Lol

Funny, is it not!!

Lol.Very...spooky, too

Could have shared one ☺

Hahaha

Lol yes true

Not bloody sleepy

Cannot believe it

Lol! Me neither, and it should be; it's so late!

Just past that point when it's late enough to get reenergized

I was asleep on the table at 10!!

Lol! Well, you will need energy to drive a quad ;) But we could go for a pajama walk if you like...

Yes

Lol

I have no PJ

Lol

Can wear jeans

Va bene lol

Since it's fresh

To be outside

But Beautiful

For sure

Ok 10 mins

Ok, lol c u outside

Walk towards the beach, and there are two loungers on the sand.

Perfect ☺

When I got there, he offered to share one lounger. We cuddled while he told me stories about Malta. After a few shooting stars, finally, I finally kissed him. It was the first time I can remember making a first move. It was an irresistible and inevitable consummation. In his room, in a way, it felt like we were healing each other's betrayed hearts. It was a sweet, even if a bit stereotypical, wedding hookup.

Chapter 37

MORE ITALY

Back in Florence, I did a bit more shopping but also took up my quest in search of new flavors of gelato Italian ice cream. Some favorites were cantucci, which is like a biscotti, and cinnamon or kiwi, flavors I'd never seen or tried before. On my last day, I went on a tour of Piazza Repubblica and Santa Croce with one of my favorite professors, Professoressa Ferrari, who taught me the history of Florence in Italian. She had just published an article about how ice cream was invented in Florence. As we walked, she pointed out a little shop, Vivoli, near Santa Croce, that she declared to have the best gelato in Florence. They had even recently opened a store inside Macy's in New York City. I made a note of it but didn't go. I saved it for my next trip back—and whoever might be with me.

I also got to visit with another professor, Manfredi, briefly. He was my conversation professor and is always impressed with how well I still speak Italian. I shared a nutshell version of what had been going on in my life, and he shared the Italian saying, *"Quell che non-morisse ti ingrassa."* It means what doesn't kill you is *"good"* for you. I'd have to chew on that one. I knew it rang true, but being grateful for what was done to me would take some time. It would happen more after I fully healed. All my Italian friends called JD a *"stronzo,"* and recommended I take things *"piano, piano,"* or slowly. Of course, piano, piano was also the advice I got for trying to finish off my eggplant parmesan, not just for recovering from divorce, accident, etc., so it seemed to have universal application.

I discovered the only annoying part about traveling alone was not being able to leave my bag at the table if I got up to use the restroom. It always felt like I might be dining and dashing, but no one seemed to mind if I temporarily disappeared to the toilet or for a cigarette. I never knew who I would meet while eating out. My two favorite restaurants were owned and run by two brothers, Giovanni and Nico. The guys working at La Spada, Giovanni's main gig, teased me that I was in love with Nico because I always ate at his place first, Cento Poveri. I have known Giovanni and Nico since my year studying there, and I'm lucky they treat me like family. Alone at Nico's, I kept meeting fun people at the tables next to me. I also met a couple of guys. There was a Sicilian who said he wasn't a typical Sicilian, but then, of course, he was, and he was disappointed when I later went home to my pensione instead of to his place. There was a Serbian who didn't seem to be being honest with me. He had pretended to be Italian, but we had mutual friends, so I found out his true identity—and why he didn't seem trustworthy. I stood him up one night, preferring to finish off a whole bottle of red that Renzo gave me, with a picture of his face as the David's on the bottle. I broke down into tears of relief when I learned that day via email that the bar complaint against me was dismissed. I had something more to celebrate.

As sunset neared my last day, I looked out at Florence from the small balcony of the faded pink Bardini villa and took a deep breath. I was alone on the balcony, its iron rails keeping me safe. To my surprise, it was a better panoramic view than from the touristy Piazzale Michelangelo, which I could see in the distance, just to the left of San Miniato. The sun was just about to set, and everywhere I looked was a sea of golden yellows, oranges, and reds, with white, pink, and green marble facades mixed in, all against the lush green of the surrounding hills to Fiesole and beyond.

Letting the view wash over my eyes, it was almost like meeting Florence again for the first time—but with all her history and our past shared experiences glowing from the inside. At La Spada after dinner that night, my friend Giovanni remarked how I am always sad to leave Florence. But at that moment, as the church bells rang from Santa Croce to Santa Maria Novella, I smiled. I knew it was time to go to Bali and write.

Postscript

I did learn from my first marriage that I value vows. So, I decided to write some that I would keep for myself.

I vow to myself… that from this day forward, I will live in the moment because this moment is everything. I promise to breathe deeply. I promise to laugh, to feel, to experience, and not fear any emotion that may arise because my emotions are my truth. I promise always to have at least one pet because they are perfect examples of unconditional love. Each day, my mission will be to do everything I can to keep myself happy and comfortable. I will do my best to care for my earthly body. Each night, I will rest, I will let myself heal, but I will continue to dream as wildly as possible. I vow to keep my heart and soul open to being shaped by guides, gurus, and all spiritual masters of peaceful origin. I will never forget that it is not possible to erase from existence my being, my true nature, my ultimate essence, which is love, source energy, and light. When it is my time, I will cross over to the invisible world without pain and into a welcoming, of love and of light, and I will freely merge into the immense, infinite love that awaits me, and that is already here, inside each one of us. I give thanks for the gift of my life, for the beauty of perfection, and for the gift of knowledge, through which I can only begin to appreciate the greatness of my story and through which I can only imagine all that I learn from hearing the stories of others. All of this, but especially goodness and love, freedom and adventure, do I vow to myself.

About the Author

SARAH SMALL is a lawyer who embarked on a transformative journey after being diagnosed with bipolar disorder in 2010. Her life took an unexpected turn when she discovered her husband's infidelity, which, along with ill-advised prescriptions triggered her first manic episode. In the wake of this upheaval, she made the difficult decision to leave her law practice behind and start anew.

Upon her return from Bali where this manuscript was first written, she sought solace and a fresh beginning, and she relocated to a different state, hoping to distance herself from the painful memories. However, her search for peace led her even further, ultimately prompting a move to a new country.

Despite her best efforts, the spectre of mania remained a constant foe throughout her journey. It took thirteen years of introspection, self-discovery, and personal growth after each additional debilitating episode for her to finally come to terms with her condition. Through her experiences, she has gained invaluable insights into the challenges and triumphs of living with bipolar disorder, which she now shares with others in the hopes of fostering understanding, empathy, and resilience in the face of adversity.

www.ingramcontent.com/pod-product-compliance
Lightning Source LLC
LaVergne TN
LVHW040518210926
848480LV00007BA/1501
9798234144027